Revitalizing
Higher Education

Revitalizing Higher Education

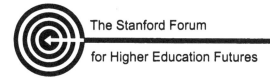

The Stanford Forum

for Higher Education Futures

**Joel W. Meyerson and William F. Massy
Editors**

Peterson's

Princeton, New Jersey

Contents

Preface

The Stanford Forum for Higher Education Futures is a national research center resident at Stanford University. Its mission is to improve the strategy, finance, and management of American colleges and universities. The Stanford Forum helps college and university officers and governing boards respond to new imperatives, develop viable institutional strategies, and implement them through effective finance and management. It conducts and sponsors research and disseminates knowledge through symposia, retreats, books, and monographs. Forum fellows include leaders and innovators in higher education and industry. The Stanford Forum is the successor to the Forum for College Financing, which was resident at Columbia University.

Introduction

William F. Massy and Joel W. Meyerson

As we prepare to enter the twenty-first century, higher education faces new challenges that can become opportunities for revitalization. If they are to thrive, the colleges and universities of tomorrow must learn to rethink their mission and invent a future that preserves the sterling achievements of the past and, at the same time, reflects the fundamental changes transforming our world.

Revitalizing Higher Education presents a series of timely and lively essays providing lessons and successful techniques—some adapted from industry, others created on campus.

In "Academic Renewal at Michigan," University of Michigan President James Duderstadt describes the modern research university as a complex corporate conglomerate in danger of diluting its core businesses. The successful university of the future, according to Duderstadt, will maintain the centrality of student learning and faculty scholarship while focusing on transforming these core functions to take advantage of new technologies and respond to changing societal needs.

Duderstadt offers ten paradigms to illustrate the kinds of changes that may be needed, and he explores how complex organizations like the University of Michigan must address the problem of transformation.

"The Future of Academic Tenure," by Richard Chait, explains that academic tenure stands on two legs: economic security and academic

1

freedom. Chait, who is Director for Higher Education Governance and Leadership and Professor of Higher Education Management at the University of Maryland, College Park, tells us that both legs are a bit wobbly these days.

The author professes that, conventional wisdom to the contrary, tenure does not appear to undermine productivity. Further, he explains that tenure has been challenged as ill-timed and ill-suited to the careers of academic women. Chait argues that the simplest approach would be to incorporate institutional need or strategic priorities as more explicit and central criteria for tenure decisions.

Richard Lester's essay entitled "Today in Higher Education" examines the implications of the wave of industrial restructuring for the academic world. Lester, Professor of Nuclear Engineering at MIT and the Founder and Director of the MIT Industrial Performance Center, explains that higher education has a two-part question to answer. The first part has to do with *how* we should be doing things. The second part deals with what these changes in industry might mean or should mean for the goals of our enterprise. He asks, "What, if anything, do they imply about *what* we are trying to accomplish?"

In "Restructuring British Higher Education," we examine one country's approach to an important new development in governmental funding for higher education—performance-based resource allocation. The author, Graeme Davies, is chief executive of the Higher Education Funding Council for England (HEFCE) and one of the principal architects of Britain's present funding system, which has stirred considerable controversy and may be a harbinger of things to come in the U.S. and elsewhere.

American educators can gain valuable insights and ideas from an examination of the recent British actions, even though differences in the two systems make direct comparisons problematical. The British funding processes' greatest applicability in American higher education obviously lies in the public sector, but independent institutions may wish to consider some of the principles for use internally.

"Applying Contribution Margin Analysis in a Research University" describes an internally developed financial statement—the Stanford Cost Model—that summarizes cost and revenue data in a format highly useful for understanding and analyzing academic programs. In contrast to many other cost analyses built around administrative processes or overhead allocations, the Stanford Cost Model focuses on academic activity—the primary "business" of the institution.

The authors, Dan Rodas, Geoffrey Cox, and Joy Mundy, explain that the model can also be used to understand and improve certain nonacademic administrative functions. Rodas is Research Assistant to the Vice Provost for Institutional Planning and Financial Affairs at Stanford University. Cox, also at Stanford, is Vice President for Planning and Financial Affairs. Mundy, formerly with Stanford, is currently Managing Director of InfoDynamics, a consulting firm.

In his essay "Going for the Baldrige: Restructuring Academic Programs," Dean Hubbard discusses the Baldrige Criteria, a tool designed to expose the extent to which certain universal characteristics of effective large-group behavior are present or absent in an organization. Hubbard, President of Northwest Missouri State University, explains how his institution began the process of incorporating the concepts and criteria of the Malcolm Baldrige National Quality Award into the University's planning process.

This move, he explains, represented an extension and refinement of Northwest's formal quality journey, which started in 1984 when the University deliberately sought to apply in education what was being tested in industrial settings. The dramatic results received nationwide attention.

It is our hope that these essays provide a context and some of the tools you'll need to shape and revitalize your institution's future at what may be the most important crossroads of its history.

Chapter 1

::

Academic Renewal at Michigan

James Duderstadt

::

Over the last year I've run a simple experiment. I've asked various groups to assess the degree of change they believe universities will undergo during the 1990s, ranked on a scale from 0 to 10, with zero as the status quo and 10, radical change. I have found that faculty generally respond with estimates of three or four—there will be change but nothing earthshaking. Academic administrators—deans, provosts, and the like—tend to believe there will be more radical change, say on the order of seven or eight on the 10-point scale. But when I ask university presidents the same question, their responses bound off the scale: their average assessment is that the magnitude of change in our institutions will be about a 20! My own sense is that's about right.

WHERE WE ARE AND HOW WE GOT HERE

Before exploring change in higher education, it is helpful to understand what the modern research university has become. Part of the dilemma is that very few people, on campus or off, know. The public tends to think of the university in a very traditional way, with students sitting in large classrooms listening to senior faculty members lecture on Shakespeare.

The faculty thinks of Oxbridge—themselves as dons and their students as serious scholars. The federal government sees just another research and development contractor or health-care provider—a supplicant for the public purse. A brief analysis of the research university's mission shows the reality is far more complex. The classic triad of education, research, and service branches extensively, as shown in Figure 1.

Let me suggest the image of the modern research university as a complex, international conglomerate of highly diverse businesses. My school, the University of Michigan (UM), for example, might be diagrammed as shown in Figure 2. With an annual budget of over $2.5 billion, "The University of Michigan, Inc." would rank roughly 200th on the Fortune 500 list. Our several campuses educate about 50,000 students at an operating cost of about $800 million a year. We are a major federal R & D laboratory with over $400 million a year in grants and contracts. We run a massive health-care company: Our medical center treated over 800,000 patients last year and our managed-care operation comprises 70,000 "managed lives."

Last December we formed a nonprofit entity, the Michigan Health Corporation, that will allow us to make equity investments in joint ventures. Through it, we will build a statewide integrated health-care system of roughly 1,500,000 subscribers—the population size we believe necessary to keep our university-owned tertiary hospitals afloat.

Figure 1. Triad Branching

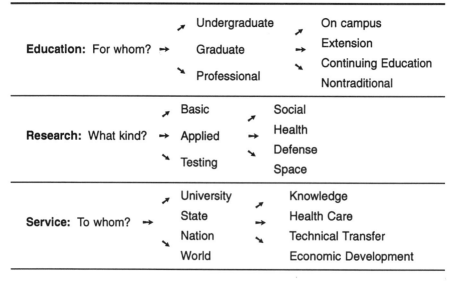

Figure 2. "The University of Michigan, Inc."

The U of M, Inc.

On-campus education	R & D	Health Care	HMO
UM Ann Arbor	$420 M	UM Medical Center	M-Care
UM Dearborn		850,000 patients	70,000 "managed lives"
UM Flint			$150 M
50,000 students		$1.2 B	
$800 M			

Insurance	Knowledge Services	Entertainment
Veritas Insurance	Continuing education	Michigan Wolverines
$200 M	Extension courses	$250 M
	Worldwide market	
	$100 B	

We also have our own captive insurance company since we are too big to buy insurance. And, we are actively involved in providing a wide array of knowledge services—from degree programs offered in Hong Kong, Seoul, and Paris to cyberspace-based activities such as managing part of the Internet. Finally, we are also involved in entertainment—the Michigan Wolverines. The $250 million under "Michigan Wolverines" in Figure 2 is not, thankfully, our athletic budget but represents licensing and everything else we do in this area. For example, recently we became the first university to sign a university-wide shoe contract with Nike, Inc., in an effort to pull in all of our various coaches' contracts.

This kind of "corporate" organization chart would describe many of the large research universities across the nation. We have all become conglomerates because of the interests and efforts of our faculty. We are prime examples of loosely coupled, adaptive systems that have grown in complexity as their various components have responded to environmental changes—each component pursuing its own particular goals. We are a "learning organization," to use the business term. Beyond that, we are also a holding company for thousands of faculty entrepreneurs.

Our character provides us with considerable resilience. Over the years we have responded to change and evolved to excel—driven by the creativity, effort, and energy of individual faculty and the units with which they identify and by a transactional culture in which everything is negotiable—"let's make a deal" writ large. Figure 3, below, describes this evolution in terms of The U of M, Inc.

But there are some problems with this reality. We may be in danger of diluting our core businesses of teaching and scholarship by engaging in so many diverse activities. And we have demonstrated a remarkable inability to eliminate outmoded and obsolete activities. Consequently, considerable underbrush clogs our enterprise even as we grow. Outdated policies, procedures, and practices increasingly stifle our best and most creative people.

As we consider change in higher education, it is important to keep in mind the extent to which the modern research university has grown and branched and the challenges it faces as a result in shaping a successful future.

THE CHALLENGE OF CHANGE

Change is nothing new to higher education. As one of civilization's most enduring institutions, the university has been quite extraordinary in its capacity to change and adapt to serve society. Far from being immutable, the university has changed considerably over time and continues to do so today. A simple glance at the remarkable diversity of institutions comprising higher education in America demonstrates this evolution.

Figure 3. Evolution of The U of M, Inc.

UM:	The U of M, Inc.:
A loosely coupled, adaptive system of growing complexity as it responds to a changing environment	• On-campus education • Research and development • Health-care • HMOs • Knowledge services • Insurance company • Entertainment

Natural evolution characterized by:
• a transactional culture
• decentralization with optimization at the level of individual units
• little attention to core mission or fundamental values

Concerns with The U of M, Inc.:
• dilution of "core businesses"
• so complex that few understand totality
• unable to eliminate outmoded and obsolete activities
• best people hindered by outdated policies, procedures, practices

The profound nature of the challenges and changes facing higher education in the 1990s compares in significance to two other periods of great change in the nature of the American university: the late nineteenth century when comprehensive public universities first appeared and the years following World War II when research universities evolved to serve the needs of postwar America.

A century ago, the industrial revolution was transforming our nation from an agrarian society into the industrial giant that would dominate the twentieth century. The original colonial colleges, based on the elitist educational principles of Oxbridge, were jointed by land-grant public universities committed to broad educational access and service to society. Higher education saw massive growth in merit-based enrollments at the undergraduate, graduate, and professional level as comprehensive universities subsequently evolved.

A similar period of rapid change occurred after World War II. The educational needs of returning veterans, the role of universities in national defense, and the booming postwar economy led to an explosion in both the size and number of major universities. So, too, the direct involvement of the federal government in the support of campus-based research led to the evolution of the research university as we know it today.

We now face challenges and opportunities similar to those of these earlier periods of transformation. Many observers focus on immediate challenges such as the rapidly growing costs of quality education and research during a period of limited resources, the erosion of public trust and confidence in higher education, or the deterioration in the relationship between research universities and the federal government. But our institutions will be affected more profoundly by powerful societal changes driving transformation: the increasing ethnic and cultural diversity of our people; the growing interdependence of nations; and the degree to which knowledge itself has become the key driving force in determining economic prosperity, national security, and social well-being.

One frequently thinks of the primary missions of the university in terms of teaching, research, and service. But these roles can also be regarded as simply the twentieth-century manifestations of the more fundamental roles of creating, preserving, integrating, transmitting, and applying knowledge. And while it is clear that these fundamental university roles have not changed over time, the way in which these missions have been realized has changed dramatically.

Consider, for example, the role of teaching (i.e., transmitting knowledge). While we generally think of a professor teaching to a classroom of students who read assigned texts, write papers, solve problems or perform experiments, and take examinations, this type of instruction is a relatively recent form of pedagogy. Throughout the last millennium, the more common form of learning was through apprenticeship. Both the neophyte scholar and craftsman learned by working as apprentices to a master. While one-on-one learning still occurs today in skilled professions such as medicine and in advanced education programs such as the Ph.D. dissertation, it is simply too labor-intensive for the mass educational needs of modern society.

The classroom itself may soon be replaced by more appropriate and efficient learning experiences. Indeed, such a paradigm shift may be forced upon the faculty by the students themselves. Today's students are members of the "digital" generation. They have spent their early lives surrounded by robust, visual, electronic media—"Sesame Street," MTV, home computers, video games, cyberspace networks, and virtual reality. They approach learning as a "plug-and-play" experience, unaccustomed and unwilling to learn sequentially—to read the manual—and rather inclined to plunge in and learn through participation and experimentation. While this type of learning is much different from the sequential, pyramid approach of the traditional university curriculum, it may be far more effective for this generation, particularly when provided through a media-rich environment.

Hence, faculty members of the twenty-first-century university could well be asked to set aside their roles as teachers to become designers of learning experiences, processes, and environments. Tomorrow's faculty may have to discard the present style of solitary learning experiences in which students tend to learn primarily on their own through reading, writing, and problem solving. Instead they may be asked to develop collective learning experiences in which students work and learn together, with the faculty member becoming more of a consultant or a coach than a teacher.

The process of research and scholarship—creating new knowledge—is also evolving rapidly away from the solitary research to scholarly teams spread over several disciplines. Indeed, is the concept of the disciplinary specialist really necessary—or even relevant—in a future where the most interesting and significant problems will require this kind of "big think" rather than "small think"? Who needs such specialists when intelligent software agents will be available to roam far and wide through robust networks containing the knowledge of the world, instantly and effortlessly extracting whatever a person wishes to know?

So, too, there is increasing pressure to draw research topics more directly from worldly experience and needs than from the curiosity of scholars. Furthermore, the nature of knowledge creation is shifting somewhat away from the analysis of what has been to the creation of what has never been—drawing more on the experience of the artist than upon analytical skills of the scientist.

The preservation of knowledge is one of the most rapidly changing functions of the university. The computer, or more precisely the digital convergence of various media, has already supplanted the printing press in impacting knowledge. For centuries the intellectual focal point of the university has been the library—civilization's knowledge preserved as a collection of written works. Yet today such knowledge exists in many forms beyond print. Text, graphics, sound, algorithms, virtual reality simulations exist literally "in the ether" as digital representations over worldwide networks, accessible to anyone, not just a privileged few in academe.

Finally, it is also clear that societal needs will continue to dictate great changes in the applications of knowledge it accepts from universities. Over the past several decades, universities have been asked to take the lead in applying knowledge across a wide array of activities—from providing health care and protecting the environment to rebuilding our cities and entertaining the public at large (although it is sometimes hard to understand how intercollegiate athletics represents knowledge application!).

Here we face a particular dilemma. The pace of change has become so rapid and the nature of change so profound that it becomes increasingly difficult to even sense the changes (although we certainly feel the consequences), much less understand them sufficiently to respond and adapt. Institutions such as universities and government agencies, which have been the traditional structures for intellectual pursuits, may turn out to be as obsolete and irrelevant to the future as the American corporation of the 1950s. There is clearly a need to explore new social structures capable of sensing and understanding change and engaging in the strategic processes necessary to adapt to or control it.

SOME DIFFERENT PARADIGMS

To illustrate the profound nature of this challenge, it is interesting to consider new paradigms that might characterize the "university of the twenty-first century." Several of the more provocative are described below.

Of course, our institutions are unlikely to assume the form of any one of these models. But, as the diagram of a possible twenty-first-century university in Figure 4 shows, each paradigm reflects aspects that almost certainly will be a part of our character in the century ahead.

These paradigms suggest the extraordinary nature of the transformations that will be required in our universities in the years ahead. Just as they have so many times in the past, our institutions must continue to change and evolve if we are to continue to serve—and, indeed, remain relevant to—a rapidly changing world.

SOME LESSONS LEARNED

So how does an institution as large, complex, and tradition-bound as the modern research university go about transforming itself? Historically we

Figure 4. A Vision of the 21st Century University

START WITH THE FUNDAMENTALS

- Attract, retain, and sustain outstanding people
- Achieve and enhance academic excellence
- Optimize quality, breadth, scale, excellence, and innovation
- Retain sufficient autonomy to control own destiny
- Balance resource portfolio to support excellence
- "Keep the joint jumpin' "

CORE VALUES	ELEMENTS OF THE VISION	PARADIGMS BASED ON THE VISION
Excellence	Excellence and leadership	The Creative University
Leadership	Turning dreams into reality	The New University
Critical Inquiry	A relish for innovation and	The Cyberspace University
Liberal learning	excitement	The Knowledge Server
Diversity	Control of our own destiny	The Divisionless University
Caring and concern	Freedom and responsibility of	The Lifelong University
Community	students and faculty	The World University
Creativity	Diverse in character yet united	The University College
Innovation	in values	The Hybrid Public-Private
	A center of critical inquiry	University
	and learning	The Diverse University
	A broad and liberal spirit	
	An uncommon education for the	
	common man	
	An independent critic and servant	
	of society	

have accomplished change using a variety of mechanisms: i) "buying" change with additional resources; ii) laboriously building the consensus necessary for grassroots support of change; iii) changing key people; iv) finesse; v) by stealth of night; and vi) "Just do it!"—that is, top-down decisions followed by rapid execution (following the old adage that "it is better to seek forgiveness than to ask permission").

But we will need a more strategic approach to stay the course while moving our institutions toward the paradigms likely to characterize higher education in the years ahead. Indeed, many institutions have already embarked on major transformation agendas similar to those characterizing the private sector. Some even use familiar language: "transforming," "restructuring," or even "reinventing" their institutions. But, of course, herein lies one of the great challenges to universities. Since our various missions and our diverse array of constituencies give us a complexity far beyond that encountered in business or government, the process of institutional transformation is necessarily more complex.

Based on the experiences of both public- and private-sector organizations, several features of the transformation process should be recognized at the outset:

1. The real challenge in transforming is not usually financial or organizational, but cultural. Universities will need to transform a rigid set of habits, thoughts, and arrangements currently incapable of responding to change either rapidly or radically enough.
2. True participation by key players in the design and implementation of the transformation process is essential. In the case of the university, special attention must be paid to involving the faculty—changing their culture will be the biggest challenge of all.
3. The use of an external group provides credibility to the transformation process. It is not only helpful but sometimes essential when putting controversial issues on the table (e.g., tenure reform).
4. It often takes a crisis for people to seriously consider transformation—and sometimes even this is not sufficient. Unfortunately, no universities—and few organizations in the private sector—have been able to achieve major change through the motivation of opportunity and excitement alone.

TEN PARADIGMS FOR THE 21st CENTURY UNIVERSITY

1. **The Hybrid Public-Private University:**
A state-related but independent university that has a strong public character but is supported primarily through resources it generates itself (e.g., tuition, federal grants, private giving, auxiliary enterprises).
   Key questions:
   - How does one preserve the public character of a privately financed institution?
   - How does a state-related university adequately represent the interests of its majority stockholders (parents, patients, federal agencies, donors)?
   - Can one sustain an institution of the size and breadth of our public universities on self-generated ("private") revenues alone?

2. **The World University:**
A university that adapts to the emerging global culture and services worldwide demand for learning, albeit within the context of a particular geographical area (e.g., North America).
   Key questions:
   - What would be the mission and character of a world university?
   - Who, how, where would it teach?
   - What programs would it stress? How would they be organized?
   - What strategic alliances could be formed with other institutions?
   - Would this paradigm be compatible with our state and national missions?

3. **The Diverse University (or "Transversity"):**
A university that draws its intellectual strength and character from the rich diversity of humankind, providing a model for society of a pluralistic learning community in which people respect and tolerate diversity even as they live, work, and learn together as a community of scholars.
   Key questions:
   - What society should we strive to represent? The state? The nation? The world? The present? The future?
   - What kind of diversity do we seek? Racial? Ethnic? Gender? Socioeconomic? Geographical? Intellectual? Political?
   - How do we draw strength from diversity?
   - How do we attempt to unite a diverse community?

4. **The Cyberspace University:**
A university that links students, faculty, graduates, and knowledge resources throughout the world (and possibly even beyond) via a robust digital information network.
   Key questions:
   - Will the cyberspace university be localized in space and time or will it be a "meta structure" involving many people throughout their lives, wherever they may be?
   - Is the concept of the specialist (disciplines or professions) likely to remain relevant in such a knowledge-rich environment?
   - Will lifestyles in the academy (and elsewhere) become increasingly nomadic, with people living and traveling where they wish, taking their work and social relationships with them?
   - Will knowledge become less of a resource and more of a medium in such a university?

5. **The Creative University:**
A university that has shifted its primary focus from analytical disciplines and professions to creative activities (e.g., synthesizing materials atom by atom, genetically engineering new life forms, generating artificial intelligence or virtual reality by computer) as a result of technological advances that make analysis less challenging and sophisticated creativity tools more available.
   Key questions:
   - Will the "creative" disciplines and professions (e.g., art, music, architecture, engineering) acquire more significance?
   - How does one nurture and teach the art and skill of creation?

6. **The Divisionless University:**
A more integrated, less specialized university that will evolve out of a growing perception among younger faculty that current disciplinary (and professional) structures are irrelevant to teaching,

scholarship, and service activities. The divisionless university will use webs of virtual structures to provide both horizontal and vertical integration among disciplines and professions.

Key questions:
- Should we reverse the trend toward more specialized undergraduate degrees in favor of a "bachelor's of liberal learning"?
- Has the Ph.D. itself become obsolete to the extent that it produces highly specialized clones of the present graduate faculty?
- Should the basic disciplines be mixed among the professions? Many of the most exciting problems have always been generated through interaction with the "real world."
- How do we develop, evaluate, and reward faculty who are generalists rather than specialists?

7. The University College:
A unit within the complex environment of a comprehensive research university that represents an intensified focus on undergraduate education. It will draw creatively on the intellectual resources of the entire university: its scholars, libraries, museums, liberal programs, and its remarkable diversity of people, ideas, and endeavors.

Key questions:
- Should we shift from solitary to collective learning experiences?
- How do we respond to the fact that the current generation of students is quite different from the faculty, both in cultural composition and styles of learning (e.g., the "plug and play" generation)?
- Should we require all faculty on our campuses—including those from professional schools—to become involved in undergraduate education?

8. The Lifelong University:
A university that addresses the entire continuum of education, from cradle to grave. It may form strategic alliances with other components of the educational system and commits to lifetime interaction with its students, providing them with the continuing education necessary to meet their evolving goals and needs.

Key questions:
- How would this lifetime education be delivered?
- How would the university relate to other components of the educational continuum?
- How would this "seamless web" approach relate to our current focus on well-defined degree programs?

9. The New University:
A "university" within a university that serves as a laboratory for prototyping and testing innovative academic applications. This academic unit of students, faculty, and programs will provide the intellectual and programmatic framework for continual experimentation that helps shape the vision and refine the features of the future university.

Key questions:
- Should the New U be a laboratory or proving ground for various possible visions of the university, or should it be a more permanent part of the university that we try to keep 20 or 30 years ahead of its time?
- Would the New U be a physical or virtual structure?
- Should the New U be built around research or service?
- How would we select students and faculty for the New U?

10. The Knowledge Server:
A university that broadly and innovatively defines its role as knowledge server—creating, preserving, transmitting, and applying knowledge—by forging beyond traditional twentieth-century notions of teaching, research, and service to embrace new approaches and technologies (e.g., digital convergence, collective learning, strategic research).

Key questions:
- Is the paradigm of classroom teaching only a temporary device for learning? After all, the apprenticeship model has dominated for most of the last millennium.
- What are the implications of digital convergence, which will provide the knowledge of the world in many forms—text, graphics, sound, algorithms, virtual reality simulations—distributed over worldwide networks accessible by anyone?
- Will our institutions be asked by society to take on new roles that respond to new priorities (e.g., economic competitiveness and global change)?

5. The organizational head must play a critical role as both leader and educator in designing, implementing, and selling the transformation process. University presidents in this role should particularly engage faculty in the process.

Experience demonstrates that organizational transformation is not only possible but even predictable to a degree. The revolutionary process starts with an analysis of the external environment and the recognition that radical change is the organization's best response to the challenges it faces. The early stages are sometimes turbulent—marked by conflict, denial, and resistance—but gradually, leaders and members of the organization begin to develop a shared vision of what their institution should become and turn their attention to the transformation process. In the final stages, grass-roots incentives and disincentives are put into place, creating internal market forces that drive institutional change. Methods are also developed that measure the success of the transformation process. Ideally, the process never ends.

The necessary transformation should go far beyond simply restructuring finances to face the brave new world of limited resources. Rather, they should encompass every aspect of our institutions, including:

- the mission of the university
- financial restructuring
- organization and governance
- general characteristics of the university
- intellectual transformation
- relations with external constituencies
- cultural change

Universities, like most large, complex, and hierarchical organizations, tend to become bureaucratic, conservative, and resistant to change. Over time we have become encrusted with policies, procedures, committees, and organizational layers that tend to discourage risk-taking and creativity. We must take decisive action to streamline processes, procedures, and organizational structures to enable our institutions to better adapt to a rapidly changing world.

CONCLUSION

There is an increasing sense among American higher education's leaders and constituencies that the 1990s will represent a period of significant change on the part of our universities. If we are to respond successfully to the challenges, opportunities, and responsibilities before us, we will need to develop the capacity to transform ourselves using entirely new paradigms that better serve a rapidly changing society and a profoundly changing world.

We must seek to remove the constraints that prevent our institutions from responding promptly and flexibly. We must eliminate unnecessary processes and administrative structures, question existing premises and arrangements, and challenge, excite, and embolden the members of our university communities to embark on this great adventure. Our challenge is to work together to provide an environment in which such change is regarded not as a threat but as an exhilarating opportunity to engage in the primary activity of a university: learning—in all its many forms—to better serve our world.

The remarkable resilience of our institutions, their capacity to adapt to change, has existed in the past because in many ways they are intensely entrepreneurial, transactional cultures. We have provided our faculty the freedom, the encouragement, and the incentives to move toward their personal goals in highly flexible ways, and they have done so through good times and bad. Unfortunately, their efforts have frequently led today to organizations that are too comprehensive, complex, and detached from their core mission of learning.

The challenge is to tap this great source of creativity and energy associated with entrepreneurial activity in a way that preserves our fundamental mission and values. In a sense we need to continue to encourage our tradition of natural evolution that has been so successful in responding to a changing world, but do so with greater strategic intent. Rather than continuing to evolve as an unconstrained transactional entrepreneurial culture, we need to guide this process to preserve our core missions, characteristics, and values. This strategic natural evolution of the university is described in the series of visions presented in Figure 5.

We must also develop greater capacity to redirect our resources toward our highest priorities. While we are facing a period of more constrained resources, I believe that most of our institutions will continue to grow. After all, the knowledge business is a "growth industry." Yet, to use a gardening analogy, we need to develop the capacity to prune and shape this growth so that it is more strategic.

In summary, I share the sense among most of my colleagues as presidents of universities that the 1990s will see extraordinary changes in

Figure 5. Strategic Natural Evolution of the University

UM:
A loosely coupled, adaptive system of growing complexity as it responds to a changing environment

The U of M, Inc.:
- On-campus education
- Research and development
- Health-care
- HMOs
- Knowledge services
- Insurance company
- Entertainment

Vision 1995:
Continued evolution as an unconstrained, transactional, entrepreneurial culture

Vision 2000:
Excellence and leadership . . . position UM for leadership within the existing paradigm of the research university

Vision 2017:
Strategic natural evolution . . .

. . . attract, retain, and empower exceptionally creative people capable of exploring new paradigms

. . . develop the capability to discontinue obsolete or extraneous activities

. . . with constraints, preserve core missions, character, and fundamental values

Natural evolution characterized by:
- a transactional culture
- decentralization with optimization at the level of individuals units
- little attention to core mission or fundamental values

Concerns with The U of M, Inc.:
- dilution of "core businesses"
- so complex that few understand totality
- unable to eliminate outmoded and obsolete activities
- best people hindered by outdated policies, procedures, practices

the nature of higher education and the nature of our institutions. A key element will be to provide ourselves with the flexibility and capacity to change in order to serve a changing society. But we must change in such a way that we preserve fundamental aspects of our characters and our values. This capacity for change—for renewal—is the key objective that we have to strive for in the years ahead. As the university has done many times in the past, it must transform itself again to meet the future.

Chapter 2

::

The Future of Academic Tenure

Richard P. Chait

::

For most of the twentieth century, tenure has been a prominent, prevalent, and durable feature of the academic landscape. Consider the following statistics.

- Seventy-one percent of all institutions have a tenure system.[1]
- Faculty on campuses with tenure systems comprise 81 percent of all full-time faculty.
- Despite all the concerns about an ossified, overly tenured faculty, the proportion of faculty with tenure has changed little over the past decade. National Center for Education Statistics data indicate the following: 64.8 percent of faculty were tenured in 1980–81, 66 percent in 1985–86, 64.9 percent in 1987-88, and 63.4 percent in 1992–93 (Figure 1).
- The percentage of women with tenure increased slightly during the 1980s. According to the EEOC, 55.7 percent of women faculty were tenured in 1979 and 59.2 percent in 1989. Nearly 72 percent of male professors were tenured in 1979 and 74.9 percent in 1989.

---

[1] "Institutional Policies Regarding Faculty in Higher Education," National Center for Higher Education Statistics, 1987 data, reported January 1990.

Figure 1. Full-Time Instructional Faculty with Tenure,
1980–81 and 1992–93

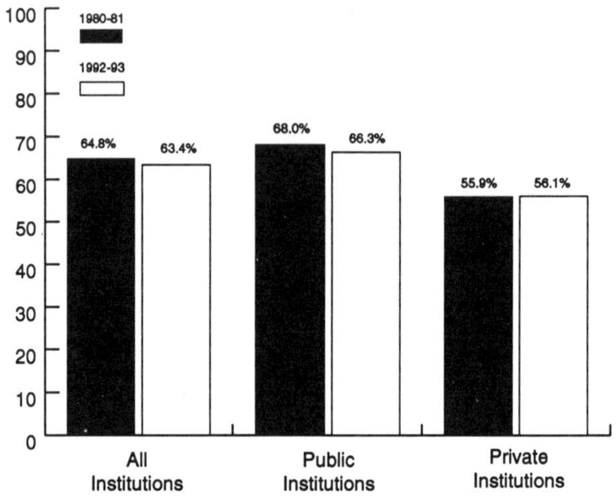

This survey included institutions with and without tenure systems.

Source: U.S. Department of Education, National Center for Education Statistics, *Faculty Salaries, Tenure, and Fringe Benefits*; and Integrated Postsecondary Education Data System (IPEDS), "Salaries, Tenure, and Fringe Benefits of Full-Time Instructional Faculty" surveys. (This table was prepared in October 1993.)

- Slightly more than half (54 percent) of all faculty surveyed in 1989 considered tenure more difficult to achieve than five years earlier. In 1986–87, when 16 percent of all tenure-track faculty were considered for tenure, 79 percent of those decisions were favorable.
- The percentage of institutions with tenure quotas has not changed dramatically. It remains at about 13 percent of all colleges and universities.
- Six percent of all colleges and universities have tenure systems for part-time faculty.

THE PUBLIC CONTEXT

Attacks on academic tenure periodically erupt. The last major assault was in the late 1960s and early 1970s, when state legislators, disenchanted with campus activists and student demonstrations, concluded that faculty radicals were beyond accountability and reproach. Of the many legislative initiatives advanced, however, only one was enacted, and that affected only community colleges in Virginia.

The impetus for reform in the 1990s, however, does not rest on revenge or retribution. The dominant motives now are managerial and practical, and concerns about tenure extend to the boardrooms of private colleges as well as the halls of state legislatures.

Academic tenure stands on two legs: economic security and academic freedom. Both legs are a bit wobbly these days because the context for the debate about tenure *is* different.

First, the very notion of economic security has become anachronistic throughout corporate America. Massive layoffs are routine: 38,500 employees have been laid off at IBM; 69,000 at General Motors (including 18,000 white-collar workers); 33,500 at AT&T; 31,000 at Boeing; and 13,000 at F. W. Woolworth (*New York Times,* March 22, 1994). Similar examples abound. Nationwide in 1993, twenty-nine companies eliminated at least 5,000 positions. In all, some 450,000 workers were terminated, a number nearly equal to the entire full-time faculty in the United States.

In the midst of such large-scale dislocation, the *New York Times* deemed newsworthy the University of Pennsylvania's decision to eliminate three departments (religious studies, American civilization, and regional science) and reassign the fifteen affected faculty members to other departments (October 14, 1993). Although there were to be no layoffs, reaction, nonetheless, was vocal. The *Chronicle of Higher Education* reported of the same incident that "professors are protesting the recommendations. As many as 150 showed up . . . to discuss the proposals." According to one of the target department heads, "The proposal marks the end of collegial government at Penn."

At San Diego State University, the reaction to proposed layoffs was so severe that the administration was forced to retreat. And in Canada, where unemployment is more widespread than in the United States, the president of the confederation of faculty associations commented about the disparity between industrial layoffs and the economic security of faculty. "You can't just say the university is in fiscal trouble so we'll lay off people. You have to prove that a particular job is no longer needed." A colleague at York University in Toronto added, "I acknowledge there haven't been (the) job losses in universities that there have been in other sectors, but I don't know if the logic prevails that universities must become as badly off as everybody else" (*Alberta Report*, August 23, 1993).

Even the most sympathetic supporters of higher education will be hard-pressed to defend lifetime appointments that are virtually impervious to dismissal irrespective of economic conditions, revenue shortfalls, or market demand. Juxtaposed against pervasive corporate cutbacks, especially of white-collar workers, permanent employment for professors stands in sharp relief and presents a formidable public-relations challenge. Why is tenure necessary? Why do academics require such an extraordinary measure of economic security?

The principled answer to these questions always has been "to ensure academic freedom." Yet this—the second leg of tenure—buckles too. On one hand, numerous high-profile controversies about "political correctness" have raised the issue of academic freedom. Recent well-publicized cases have included Anita Hill at the University of Oklahoma, Michael Levin and Leonard Jeffries at the City University of New York (CUNY), Tony Martin at Wellesley College, protests directed against Christie Farnham Pope, a white woman teaching African-American history at the University of Iowa, and pressures on medical schools not to teach abortion procedures. In public school systems, teachers have been directed to include creationism as well as evolution in the science curriculum, and for a brief time in Lake County, Florida, teachers were instructed to assert the superiority of American culture to all other societies.

Regardless of how much academics may wish these threats to academic freedom would offset criticisms of tenure, the reverse may be true. Especially with respect to matters of "political correctness," many trustees, legislators, and citizens believe academic freedom actually *enables* faculty to offer unsubstantiated conclusions and pernicious perspectives with utter impunity. In other words, were it not for academic tenure, professors would have to be *more* intellectually rigorous and *more* professionally responsible.

In addition, the forcefulness of the academic freedom argument has been weakened by the habitual and often successful resort to litigation by faculty who contend their right to unfettered expression has been abridged. To cite only two instances, the courts reinstated Leonard Jeffries, who alleged he had been removed as department chair in African-American studies at CUNY in retaliation for controversial (critics claim "racist") remarks he made about whites, and in particular, Jews; and a professor at the University of New Hampshire, whose language in the classroom was regarded by some women to be offensive and tantamount to sexual harassment, likewise was awarded reinstatement and damages by a federal district court (*New York Times,* December 4, 1994). Decisions such as these persuade the public that to ensure academic freedom, professors do not need an additional layer of protection above and beyond the judicial system.

THE ACADEMIC CONTEXT

In the main, questions about the legitimacy and utility of academic tenure have been raised by "outsiders," typically legislators, trustees, and the public. And while that remains the case, there has been some erosion, or at least reconsideration, of internal support for tenure.

In the face of financial hardships, increased competition for enrollments, and shifts in student demand, college and university administrators have heightened concerns about the constraints tenure imposes on programs. As William F. Massy, professor and former chief financial officer at Stanford University, commented at the 1994 Stanford Forum for Higher Education Futures, tenured faculty enjoy a considerable measure of freedom to pursue interests and other activities to satisfy personal or professional goals that may not necessarily conform to institutional strategy. To align the preferences of tenured faculty and the priorities of the organization (for example, to bolster general education or improve the quality of instruction), campus leaders often must rely upon personal persuasion or material inducements.

In a shriller voice, Martin Anderson, senior fellow at the Hoover Institution at Stanford University, echoes Massy's concern:

> There is little a president of a university can command; he must cajole and persuade. In most matters concerning teaching and research, the professorial dukes of academia treat the administrators with amused disdain, for they know better than anyone the near invulnerability of their tenured posts.[2]

---

[2] *Impostors in the Temple,* Simon & Schuster, 1992, p. 194.

Objections to tenure leveled by administrators are, perhaps, to be expected. Less predictably, some faculty have joined the chorus of critics. Among the most vocal detractors are members of new populations within the academy. There are several reasons for their dissent. Despite more than twenty years of affirmative action, the percentages of all minority faculty and tenured minority faculty are virtually unchanged. The percentage of African-American faculty at predominantly white colleges is unchanged since 1979 at 2.3 percent. The percentage of tenured African Americans has increased modestly from 58.4 percent to 61 percent, and the proportion of tenured Hispanics has increased slightly from 62.1 percent to 63.9 percent[3] (Figure 2). Some members of protected classes regard tenure, coupled with the end to mandatory retirement, as a major impediment to affirmative action insofar as lifetime appointments constrain turnover and thereby foreclose opportunities to diversify the faculty.

Tenure has also been challenged as ill-timed and ill-suited to the careers of academic women. In an op-ed article in the *New York Times,* Shirley Tilghman, a professor of microbiology at Princeton University, decried her objection to tenure:

> The problem of reconciling a scientific career with some semblance of a normal life is exacerbated by the tenure system. A woman is usually 30 years of age before assuming an assistant professorship at a university, which puts her tenure decision at age 35 to 36. Thus, her critical scientific years, in which she is establishing her reputation, and her peak reproductive years coincide. This is a dirty trick . . . I favor abolishing tenure entirely in favor of rolling appointments that are regularly reviewed. Tenure is no friend to women. It does not protect them from institutional discrimination. Rather it rigidifies their career path when they need maximum flexibility.—(January 26, 1993)

Many women and minorities from the University of California to the Ivy League have asserted that the veil of confidentiality conceals bias and prejudice and severely limits a candidate's ability to understand the "true" reasons for promotion and tenure decisions. As Caroline Heilbron of Columbia University stated after she deliberately disclosed privileged information, ". . . in my experience, confidentiality means complicity,

---

[3] Jeffrey F. Milem and Helen S. Astin, "The Changing Composition of the Faculty," *Change,* March/April 1993.

Figure 2. Full-Time Faculty Tenure Rates by Gender and Race/Ethnicity, 1979 and 1989

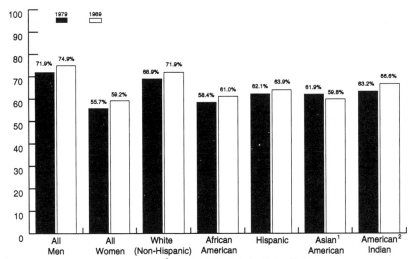

¹ Asian American includes Pacific Islanders.   ² American Indian includes Alaskan Natives.

Note: Tenure rates are based on the number of full-time faculty on "tenure track," and therefore exclude faculty who are in nontenure-earning positions. Employment counts are based on the following number of higher education institutions each year: 2,879 in 1979; 3,011 in 1983; 2,868 in 1985; and 3,452 in 1989. Data are based on reported counts and are not imputed for nonreporting institutions.

Source: U.S. Equal Employment Opportunity Commission, "EEO-6 Higher Education Staff Information" Surveys, 1979, 1983, 1985, and 1989.

useful chiefly for protecting old-boy secrets" (*New York Times Sunday Magazine,* November 8, 1992). Perceptions of inequities created by the secrecy and inflexibility of the tenure process have contributed to the erosion of support for the concept within the profession. In a survey of more than 5,000 faculty on the *Condition of the Professoriate,* 29 percent of all faculty, 32 percent of women faculty, and 39 percent of faculty under age 39 agreed that "the abolition of tenure would, on the whole, improve the quality of American higher education" (Carnegie Foundation for the Advancement of Teaching, 1989).

As confirmation that politics does indeed produce strange bedfellows, the chorus of criticisms about tenure by minorities and women has been echoed by the academic "right." Thus, Martin Anderson's *Impostors in the Temple* listed the abolition of tenure as among the ten most crucial steps to improve higher education.

Tenure is corrupting; it gives academic intellectuals almost unlimited license to do as they please with no fear of consequences. Its major effect is to encourage sloth. . . . Whatever tenuous justifications existed for establishing tenure some 50 years ago are gone, and the corrupting influence of a guaranteed job for life far outweighs any arguments in support of the idea. . . . (T)he future of American education belongs to those who are good enough to keep their jobs on the basis of performance (pp. 121, 207).

As Richard M. Huber, former dean of Hunter College, declared in *How Professors Play the Cat Guarding the Cream,* "The purpose of tenure is protection of intellectual freedom; the consequence is job security. . . . How about substituting long-term contracts? Ten years is a sensible term. It's a fair way of increasing personnel flexibility while getting rid of ineffectual teachers."[4] Academics should not dismiss these broadsides—however shrill—since these indictments do, in fact, catch the attention and shape the views of policy makers in legislatures and boardrooms, probably far more than well-footnoted studies on the subject.

THE TRENDS

To summarize, the conventional case for tenure—economic security and academic freedom—strikes many policy makers and citizens as an antiquated argument for undue privilege. And within the academy, different voices for different reasons have intensified the debate about tenure's value and utility.

Has anything changed as a result? I would like to describe three emergent trends and then speculate about the future.

Less confidentiality, more openness

Unquestionably, the cornerstone of confidentiality has been blasted away. The courts repeatedly have granted investigatory agencies access to confidential materials and to the files of comparables (previous candidates similarly situated). This principle was firmly established by the U.S. Supreme Court in 1990 in *University of Pennsylvania v. EEOC.*[5]

---

[4] George Mason University Press, 1992, p. 27.
[5] 10 S.Ct 577, p. 584.

Moreover, several state courts have affirmed a candidate's right to inspect his or her entire dossier. As the Ohio State Supreme Court ruled in *State ex. rel. James v. Ohio State University* last year, "It seems the antithesis of academic freedom to maintain secret files upon which promotion and tenure decisions are made, unavailable even to the person who is the subject of the evaluation."[6]

In recognition of these legal realities, the University of California System decided to provide candidates with all records of internal deliberations and external letters of reference with only the signature blocks and letterheads redacted. This policy applies to all personnel decisions, including promotion and tenure, merit pay, and applications for sabbatical leaves. In a 1991 memorandum to William R. Frazer, senior vice president of the University of California, Berkeley, the Committee on Affirmative Action of the U.C. System and the Association of Academic Women at Berkeley applauded the end to "clandestine confidentiality that creates doubt and suspicion" and the onset of great openness and impartial reviews able to withstand intense scrutiny. At the University of Alaska, where deliberations by governmental agents must be open, every candidate for promotion or tenure has the right to observe all committee meetings where recommendations are formulated.

Some traditionalists, such as Berkeley's Martin Trow, hold the opposite perspective. Trow contends that openness will mute sharp distinctions and blunt the meritocratic dimensions of review.[7] Others believe openness will reduce the degree of participation and candor by internal and external referees.

Personnel decisions based on actual precedents, not published standards

At least two decisions at Berkeley established that the threshold for tenure would *not* be the criteria and standards specified in the faculty handbook but the actual records and performance of male counterparts. Likewise, the Supreme Court's ruling in the *University of Pennsylvania* case upheld the right of the EEOC to assess the qualifications of five male comparables to determine if the university discriminated against a

---

[6] 1994, 70 Ohio St. 3d 168.

[7] Richard P. Chait, "University of California System [A]," Harvard Graduate School of Education, Institute for Educational Management, 1992, p. 13.

female candidate for tenure. In a unanimous decision, the court declared, "Indeed, if there is a 'smoking gun' to be found that demonstrates discrimination in tenure decisions, it is likely to be tucked in peer-review files."

This creates a *very* different yardstick for promotion and tenure decisions and foretells a significant shift in the applicable standard of measurement—a change from policy to practice, from words to deeds. Furthermore, these decisions suggest that any changes, especially efforts to tighten standards for promotion and tenure—a step taken by 21 percent of all institutions surveyed in 1988 by the National Center for Education Statistics (NCES)—should be stated explicitly with due notice and applied uniformly and scrupulously.

Broader definition of scholarship

A third trend concerns the redefinition of the archetypal faculty member. In *Scholarship Reconsidered,* Ernest L. Boyer challenged the usefulness of a monolithic notion of the faculty, proposing instead that the academy recognize different forms of scholarship: discovery, application, integrating, and teaching.

Currently, there appears to be less certainty about the qualities and characteristics of scholarship—about what should count. The debate is most pronounced in newer fields (ethnic studies, women's studies, interdisciplinary fields, for example) but is also is evident in such areas as agricultural extension, the arts, and continuing education. Representative of the redefinition of scholarship, the University of California System adopted the following important policy change:

> (D)ue consideration must be given to variations among fields and specialties in appropriate outlets for publication and presentation of scholarly and other creative contributions. Contributions and achievements in such endeavors should be evaluated according to criteria appropriate to the genre and should encompass qualitatively new areas of inquiry and scholarship of *application,* as well as scholarship of discovery, that rest at the intersection of existing disciplines and areas of creative activity.[8]

---

[8] Report of the University-wide Task Force on Faculty Rewards, June 26, 1991, p. 17.

FORECASTS

There are four reasonably safe predictions and two long shots about what the future may hold for academic tenure.

More flexible tenure tracks

There will be increased flexibility to accommodate the special concerns and considerations of women, such as "stop the clock" probationary periods, more part-time positions with tenure, and more non-tenure-track positions with later conversion to the tenure track. Eventually, these options may extend to all faculty, irrespective of age or gender, who have familial responsibilities for children or parents.

More post-tenure performance reviews

Formal, systematic, periodic evaluations of tenured faculty will become more commonplace, prodded by professional and disciplinary associations, boards of trustees, and legal counsel. The University of California System reviews tenured assistant and associate professors for salary reviews and promotions every two years and full professors every three years, according to a 1991 study by the National Research Council.[9]

There probably will be an accelerated effort to develop teaching portfolios and other document-based records of performance to fatten the personnel folder for future reference. Nonetheless, assessments will *rarely* culminate in dismissal for incompetence, a fate that currently befalls an estimated fifty professors per year (*Chronicle of Higher Education,* December 7, 1994). (Symptomatic of the byzantine procedures to terminate for cause, the University of California faculty could not even agree on a definition of "incompetence.") Post-tenure reviews will emphasize faculty development and create the illusion of summative evaluations in an attempt to mollify tenure's critics.

More non-tenure-track faculty

There will be a greater reliance on part-time, adjunct, clinical, and other non-tenure-track faculty, particularly in disciplines oversupplied with

---

[9] *Ending Mandatory Retirement for Tenured Faculty,* 1991, p. 61.

qualified personnel and in the professions where practitioners are perceived to add value to the faculty mix. This cadre of faculty will provide the "cut-back cushion." In "Higher Education Staff Information," the EEOC reported that from 1981-91, the number of full-time non-tenure-track appointments expanded by 42 percent to almost 143,000 positions, and the number of part-timers grew to a total of some 300,000, an increase of 70,000 from ten years ago. This trend will continue because part-time appointments afford institutions favorable economics and programmatic latitude (Figure 3).

Status quo at elites, reform at less selective institutions

There will be no dramatic changes in the fundamental tenure provisions at prominent research universities, flagship campuses of state systems, and elite liberal arts colleges. Even to contemplate such a change would be political suicide for campus leaders. Moreover, any institution that blazed this trail likely would face an insurmountable disadvantage in the

Figure 3. Growth in Tenure-Track vs. Non-Tenure-Track Faculty, 1981–91

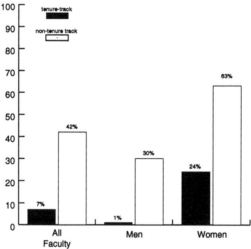

Note: Employment counts are based on the following number of higher education institutions for each year: 3,032 in 1981 and 3,285 in 1991. Data are based on reported counts and are not imputed for nonreporting institutions.

Source: U.S. Equal Employment Commission, "EEO-6 Higher Education Staff Information" Surveys, 1981 and 1991.

competition for junior and senior faculty. A change of this magnitude would require a level of collusion among peer institutions that would render petty the federal antitrust investigation of student financial aid.

Perhaps even more persuasive, there is no compelling evidence that elite institutions have been ill-served by traditional tenure systems. Conventional wisdom to the contrary, tenure does not appear to undermine productivity. A 1991 NCES study of 8,400 faculty at more than 400 institutions concluded, "The data provide no evidence of a decline in research productivity with increasing rank or with the achievement of tenure." In the two years preceding the study, professors produced more refereed articles, books, and monographs than assistant professors or nontenured faculty, and about the same number as associate professors. In the same two-year period, as well as over entire careers, "tenured faculty produced equivalent or greater numbers of all kinds of publications than tenure-track and non-tenure-track colleagues."

Smaller scale studies conducted in 1968 and 1969 reached similar conclusions. "Those who were producing kept producing; those who were turning out little continued in much the same way." The results of a broader survey in 1974 provide further evidence.

> The relationship of productivity with respect to time is not a linear function of age. Nor is it negatively correlated to career stage. The producers and the contributors maintain an output quite independent of rank or age. Hence, tenure seems not to be a causal factor. . . . (T)he evidence does not support the invective that faculty with tenure cease to produce.[10]

A more extensive survey by Oliver Fulton and Martin Trow reported in the journal *Sociology of Education* (1974) noted no substantial difference in publication rates for faculty after age 30 except for a slight drop for faculty older than age 60; among "other than ranking institutions" the proportion of inactives not publishing begins to rise after age 50. Recent data reinforce this finding. After a 1991 comprehensive review of prior studies, the National Research Council concluded that "measures of research activity show no strong relationship with age."

---

[10] Robert Blackburn, *Tenure: Aspects of Job Security on the Changing Campus,* Southern Regional Education Board, 1972, pp. 23, 25, 31.

Equally important, an NCES study uncovered "no appreciable difference in classroom hours among tenured, tenure-track, and non-tenure-track faculty (8.8 to 9.8), but all had fewer classroom hours than faculty at institutions without tenure systems (13.5). Likewise, student contact hours did not differ appreciably across the three professorial ranks. As for performance in the classroom, at least as measured by student evaluations, the National Research Council's meta-review of the literature determined that "The only conclusion one can safely draw from these studies is that they do not show a trend. . . . [Evidence] does not indicate that the teaching ability of college and university faculty declines with age."

Would first-tier institutions be better served by a contract system that presumably promotes turnover and eliminates sinecure? Whatever promise contract systems may hold in theory, the benefits of turnover simply have not been harvested in practice. As the president of one college where such a system has been in place for nearly a quarter century allowed, "We do not have a tenure system as a policy; what we have is far worse: tenure from day one." Since the 1970s, when innovative institutions adopted contract systems, the rate of renewal and degree of security has been extraordinarily high, far higher than typical tenure systems.[11]

If there are to be significant changes in tenure systems, the most fertile ground for reform will be the less selective, financially tenuous, meagerly endowed, independent four-year colleges. At less selective four-year colleges, where the board and administration typically have relatively more leverage than their counterparts at more prestigious institutions, the drawbacks to tenure are more pronounced, and the stakes in regard to organizational survival are higher. Recent examples include the decisions to abandon "presumptive tenure" at Bennington College in Vermont and to (prospectively) eliminate tenure at The College of the Ozarks and Lindenwood College, both in Missouri. These colleges are financially fragile and tuition-dependent. The threat is not the prospect of bankruptcy so much as the reality of inflexibility and overcapacity.

Much of the contempt for tenure among trustees and administrators on these campuses can be attributed to a sense that institutions with a dire need to change programs and directions feel straitjacketed by the requirement to meet an excessively strict American Association of

---

[11] Richard P. Chait and Andrew T. Ford, *Beyond Traditional Tenure*, Jossey-Bass, 1982.

University Professors (AAUP) standard of financial exigency or program discontinuation before layoffs legitimately can proceed.

By comparison, the ability of public four-year colleges and comprehensive universities to act is limited by partisan politics, statute, the considerable force of schoolteachers' unions, and the tendency to seek uniformity within a statewide system. Research universities and elite colleges are constrained, in a peculiar sense, by the formidable influence exercised by the faculty, marketplace signals of success in the form of an overabundance of applications and a steady flow of philanthropy, the absence of fiscal crisis, and a deeply entrenched commitment to mirror the preferred paradigm of the profession.

Let's turn now to the long shots, two policy options unlikely to be adopted in the short term yet worthy of consideration for the long term—especially, though not exclusively, by financially frail independent colleges.

Inducements to forgo tenure

The first long shot is predicated on the principle of voluntary actions by individual faculty members in contradistinction to an institution-wide policy that would affect all faculty. The touchstone is *choice*. Institutions would invite individual faculty to accept various incentives to forgo or forsake tenure. For example, Webster University in Missouri offers more frequent sabbaticals at higher levels of support. Waive the right to tenure and after three one-year contracts, faculty are eligible for one semester at half pay. After five years, they are eligible for one semester and summer at full pay. Only 14 percent of Webster's faculty have opted for tenure (*New York Times,* April 20, 1994).

In a similar vein, the chairman of the board of governors of the University of Alberta proposed that the university have the option of hiring faculty on a non-tenure-track contract at higher salaries than tenured professors (*Alberta Report,* August 23, 1993). Perhaps a 10 percent to 25 percent salary differential for comparably qualified individuals would induce some faculty to relinquish eligibility for tenure. A reasonable guideline would be the shorter the contract, the greater the differential; the longer the contract, the smaller the differential. The essential element would be to attach a premium to the salaries of professors disposed to take the risks inherent in term contracts. Efforts should be encouraged to establish the "price" of tenure in the marketplace and to discover the value individual faculty attach to tenure at various career stages. "Let's make a deal" may become an alternative to tenure.

By far, the most radical variation on this theme of inducements would be to exchange economic security through tenure for economic security through "ownership"—seats on the board of trustees, for example. This arrangement parallels wage and work-condition concessions by airline employees at Northwest, TWA, and United in return for seats on the board and an equity stake.

Linking tenure to institutional needs and enrollment levels

The second long shot would attempt to align the size and distribution of the faculty with market demands. Shifts in student demand are pronounced. Business majors decreased by about 22 percent in the last two years. How does a college reallocate positions to capitalize, for instance, on the growth opportunities in physical and occupational therapy?

The simplest approach would be to incorporate institutional need or strategic priorities as more explicit and central criteria for tenure decisions. There may be an evaluation of the viability of the position as well as the qualifications of the individual. Adam Yarmolinsky, Regents Professor of Public Policy in the University of Maryland System, contemplates in a draft paper, "Tenure: Permanence and Change," that tenure would "reside in a specific program, in an academic department, in a school, or in exceptional cases, across the college or university." Presumably, a more precise locus for tenure would enhance an institution's ability to discontinue select areas and individuals and reallocate positions and resources to accommodate changes in student demand.

It also is possible that subsequent to the award of tenure, employment might be contingent on a stipulated student-to-faculty ratio or certain enrollment levels (no layoffs unless enrollments drop 10 percent or more over two years, for example). But some enrollment or capacity measure would trigger dismissals rather than a declaration of financial exigency or program discontinuation because these concepts have little application to subtler shifts in markets. Alternatively, there may be a "trip wire" composed of certain critical performance indicators that would signal the circumstances under which an institution could abrogate tenure commitments.

Admittedly, these are long shots. No one should bet the ranch on either. In the end, the safest predictions are these two: 1. Twenty years from now, the terms and conditions of faculty employment will be more familiar than strange to us. True, tenure has buckled a bit while under attack, but like a resilient boxer, tenure will recover, live to fight another day, and outlast opponents for years to come. 2. Most certainly, if the past is prologue to the future, the stream of pro and con rhetoric about tenure will continue to flow unabated as befits a practice regarded as dysfunctional by some and indispensable by others.

Chapter 3

::

Today in Higher Education

Richard Lester

::

W hat can we in the academic world learn from American industry? The question is timely. It's "in the air." It's even infusing our political life. We've had, of course, the Vice President's "Reinventing Government" manifesto—a program heavily influenced by the notion that there is much to be gained by translating the best industrial practice into the public sector. We also have the phenomenon of business people running for office not as politicians but as business people. Ross Perot was the archetype. In the last election year, we had Mitt Romney in my state, and many others around the country. There isn't really anything new about this, of course. The clear-thinking, clean-cut, successful executive versus the muddle-headed, arrogant, ethically compromised, out-of-touch career politician. The go-getter versus the deadbeat. It's a theme that has graced countless campaigns over the years. But what is different today is that these personality contrasts are heightened by a more general sense of who is up and who is down in our society—a sense of decay and failure in the performance of our public institutions and a contrasting perception of success in the business world. "The American Economy—Back on Top" ran a headline in the *New York Times* a few months ago, one of many recent reports celebrating the revitalization of the nation's industries. And just last month, the World Economic Forum in Switzerland published a report concluding that the U.S. was now the most competitive economy in the world.

THE PRESENT INDUSTRIAL SITUATION

Now I'm not particularly interested in coming to the defense of our political institutions when it comes to the questions of performance. But before we turn to the question of what we in the universities might learn from industry, it is worth spending a couple of minutes on how well our industries are really doing.

It's remarkable to think that only two or three years ago, many people were arguing that the decline of U.S. industry was irreversible. Most of us here will probably remember President Bush's ill-fated trip to Tokyo with the heads of the then-ailing Big Three automobile manufacturers. That was the famous occasion on which the President threw up in the lap of the Japanese Prime Minister at a state banquet—the "barf heard around the world," as one commentator put it, rather unkindly. Mr. Bush's illness was widely interpreted as a metaphor for the sickness of the U.S. economy as a whole and its dependence on the Japanese.

But in less than three years, perceptions have been transformed. To the Japanese, we have become, to quote one Japanese newspaper, the rising Sam in the West. Japanese businessmen are flocking to our best companies to see what they can learn. American management handbooks like "Re-engineering the Corporation" are best-sellers in Japan. And American (and Japanese) analysts now was skeptical about the effectiveness of once widely admired Japanese business practices.

What happened? Has American industry indeed staged a miraculous recovery? Or are we in for another round of the national complacency that delayed U.S. adjustment to the international economy in the 1970s and 1980s? Can we tell the difference between real changes in economic capabilities and productive performance and media hype? If there has been real improvement, can we sustain it? How will things look two years from now, when the Japanese and the Europeans have pulled out of their recessions, as they are beginning to do?

I'd like to take a minute before we get on to the business at hand to look at some alternative interpretations of the present industrial situation. One interpretation is that perhaps things were never quite as bad as they were portrayed earlier. Many of the concerns of the 1980s were fueled by competitive problems in particular sectors—cars, semiconductors, steel, machine tools, and so on. But in the aggregate, the American economy was still clearly well ahead when measured in terms of wealth and generation per capita. GDP per capita is certainly not a perfect measure of the standard of living, but on the whole it is not a bad way to compare how well different national economies are doing in this regard. Based on this measure, the U.S. wasn't doing badly compared with the Europeans and Japanese, even in the late 1980s, at the height of the concern over U.S. competitiveness.

Another interpretation is that we are allowing ourselves to be deceived a little bit by the business cycle. As my colleague Bob Solow likes to say, recessions happen, and so do recoveries. They are a fact of life, and another fact of life is that, statistically speaking, economies always look better during recoveries. The question is whether this recovery is any different from previous ones. If not, the case for optimism is correspondingly weaker. In the long run the single most important measure of an economy's performance is its productivity, because in the long run the standard of living is inextricably tied to our productivity performance. By this measure, the current recovery turns out not to be unusually strong relative to previous recoveries.

Actually, this recovery *is* different in terms of its impact on jobs and wages, and not to our advantage. In manufacturing, both wages and employment have actually fallen during the first three years of the current recovery—a quite different story from previous recoveries. Moreover, this is also the first recovery in memory in which household income has actually declined. In other words, despite all of the euphoria about business performance, there are real reasons for the uncertainty and anxiety about the economy that keep showing up in the opinion polls. This is not an artificial malaise that has been manufactured by the media.

A third interpretation of the recent improvement in performance is that it is all due to exchange rates. One of the really good pieces of news about our industrial performance during the last few years has been our improved export performance. Back in 1986, the U.S. share of the world market for manufacturing exports was about 13 percent. By 1992, it had increased to 17 percent. This is a pretty good record. All of the other industrialized countries, including Japan, had experienced falling market shares. Only the "emerging seven" economies of East Asia did better than the United States in this respect.

One reason for the strong U.S. export performance is that our firms have been trying very hard to improve their competitiveness by improving their quality and productivity and so on. But another reason, obviously, is that the dollar has dropped 60 percent against the yen during this period and by lesser but still very large amounts against other leading international currencies. This would have made U.S. goods and services more competitive even if there had been no improvement in efficiency and quality. The questions is how much has the exchange rate shift contributed to the improved export picture. This is intrinsically difficult to answer, but based on a comparison of unit labor cost trends in the industrialized countries during this period it is probably not a bad guess to say that the exchange rate shift has been responsible for about three quarters of the improvement in U.S. export competitiveness.

Now none of these interpretations is in itself sufficient to account for the current situation. At the same time, though, when taken together they suggest that the situation is not quite as rosy as one might think from the more triumphal reports of industrial resurrection in the popular press. The performance of American industry has indeed been improving, and there is surely something valuable to be learned from its recent efforts and accomplishments. But let us enter into this exercise with our eyes open.

THE LESSONS OF INDUSTRY

So what exactly can we learn? What are the implications of the wave of industrial restructuring for us in the academic world. More specifically, what is the relevance of all this to our core activities in education and research?

The question really has two parts. One has to do with *how* we should be doing things. Which of the organizational changes now under way in industry seem most applicable to the organization of the academic enterprise? The other has to do with what these changes in industry might mean or should mean for the *goals* of our enterprise. What, if anything, do they imply about *what* we are trying to accomplish?

Let's begin with the first question. There is a broad consensus today about the organizational characteristics that make for competitive business enterprises: decentralization of authority and responsibility where possible; flatter organizational structures; dedication to continuous improvement; a focus on the organization's core competencies; close relations with suppliers; close attention to customers; development of the firm's human resource assets through education and training; and so on.

Several years ago, some of these ideas were still relatively novel. But today most companies profess a belief in the virtues of these things. They have become, in a sense, the new business orthodoxy.

What seems to differentiate the successful from the less successful companies is not their cognitive grasp of the importance of each item but rather the extent to which they have implemented them in their totality—as a system.

Of course, at some level what makes for a successful apparel manufacturing operation isn't what leads to success in, say, retail banking. But across the broad range of industries the leading firms are distinguished by their recognition that there is no "silver bullet" and by their ability to move simultaneously on multiple fronts. They not only understand but also seem able to act on the idea that these individual elements—the organization of work, the character of relations with suppliers and customers, the structure of the internal organization, the commitment to training, the direction of technology and market strategies—interact with each other, that these things are in fact mutually reinforcing. In this sense, one is reminded of Anna Karenina's observation that "all happy families resemble each other; [but] each unhappy family is unhappy in its own way."

The evidence for the *systemic* nature of business practice has until recently been largely anecdotal. But there is a growing body of more rigorous evidence to support this claim.

There is also a lot of other evidence that indirectly provides further support for it by affirming the limitations and even the futility of applying individual managerial solutions in isolation. (That, incidentally, is one of the main lessons to be drawn from the large number of firms whose efforts to implement specific fixes such as Total Quality Management or benchmarking or business process reengineering have yielded, by their own account, disappointingly little.)

APPLYING SUCCESSFUL BUSINESS PRACTICES TO EDUCATION

At this point we might be inclined to say, "Well, now that we know what it really takes to succeed in industry, let us try to transfer this system of practices to our own educational environment." But a few words of caution are in order.

First, it is difficult. For every firm that can legitimately claim to have made wholesale changes along these lines, there are many others that have been much less successful because they have adopted the earlier, piecemeal approach.

Second, for all the forward-looking and visionary rhetoric that surrounds these efforts, much of the heavy lifting is really concerned with how to do better, or differently, things that are already being done or how not to do them at all. While this is important—indeed, it is often essential to a firm's survival—it also suggests a limitation of much current business thinking, which is that it doesn't really have much to say about the new directions that these enterprises should be pursuing. On this critical point there is really no substitute for effective leadership. There is no formula, no twelve-step program for anticipating and responding effectively to changes in the environment. And this is surely no less true of universities than it is of firms.

And third, there is the question of just how fungible these ideas really are. How transferable are they into the academic domain? Let's consider a few of them.

First is the idea that companies, to meet the market tests of speed and responsiveness as well as cost efficiency, must break down walls between departments and functions. A good example of this, by the way, is the experience of Chrysler, whose recent revival is in many ways the most unexpected aspect of Detroit's renaissance. What is Chrysler doing right? There are many different things, but probably the most important is that the company has begun to design cars that people actually want to buy. Moreover, it is doing so quicker than anyone else. The Chrysler Neon was developed in thirty-three months, faster even than Toyota's best performance. The key to this has been the company's ability to dismantle the barriers between the scores of functions and thousands of individuals whose expertise is required to develop a new vehicle. And many other companies are beginning to find that not only does this kind of thing allow them to do better what they were doing before but that it also opens up opportunities to do things that they previously were unable to do at all.

A second idea is that enterprises should figure out what they do best and get rid of everything else. One of America's most successful companies over the last decade—by some measures perhaps the most successful—has been the semiconductor manufacturer Intel. Its chief executive officer, Andy Grove, preaches this gospel relentlessly and practices what he preaches. One of the company's most important recent moves was its decision in 1987 to get out of the business of producing DRAM memory chips—a product it had invented fifteen years earlier. This decision was the cause of much lamentation at the time. Many people saw it as spelling the end of the American semiconductor industry. But Intel realized that it couldn't compete with the Japanese in DRAMs. So it cuts its losses and instead focused almost all of its attention on making microprocessors of PCs—where it was clearly dominant and where the profit margins were much higher. This decision paid off handsomely. Intel is today the most profitable electronics company in the world and the single most important reason why the U.S. semiconductor industry has confounded the conventional wisdom of the late 1980s and reemerged as the world's strongest today.

A third idea is the importance of focusing in a single-minded way on your customer. And, of course, there are many examples in the business literature of companies that have turned themselves around by doing this, as well as many other examples that illustrate the damaging consequences of not doing so.

Now each of these three ideas on its face seems entirely relevant to us in the university community. Who here has not at one point been frustrated by the rigid, parochial, and inflexible nature of our academic departments? At their slowness in recognizing important new developments on the edge of their disciplines? At their failure to discard old and decreasingly relevant subjects? Sometimes it seems as though the departmental structure of the universities is the biggest single obstacle to change.

And Andy Grove's insistence on pruning ruthlessly everything at which you do not excel also seems particularly apposite to the universities today, as budget pressures continue to mount and it becomes clear that some things will absolutely have to go.

And who could take issue with the proposition that we in the universities must redouble our attention to the customer?

But the truth is that these ideas aren't perfectly adapted to the academic domain. The role of disciplines in academic life is *not* exactly analogous to the role of functional departments in a business firm. In both cases we're talking about coherent, self-contained bodies of knowledge. But in the universities the disciplines also serve a pedagogical purpose—a purpose that is reflected in the meaning of the word "discipline" itself: "training that corrects, molds, or perfects the mental faculties," to quote the Webster's definition. And equally important, most disciplines are in intellectual motion; they are vehicles for advancing the forefront of knowledge. These purposes are quite distinct from the roles that functional departments play in firms.

I don't want to be misunderstood about this. I'm certainly not arguing against the place of interdisciplinary studies in the university. On the contrary, I have devoted most of my own academic career to trying to advance such things. Our Industrial Performance Center at MIT is dedicated to strengthening the linkages between science and engineering and the social sciences, because it's at the interface between these disciplines that many of the most important problems in the management of technological enterprise arise today. I would submit that interdisciplinary communities of this kind are becoming invaluable intellectual assets for our universities, as it grows increasingly apparent that the most serious problems faced by society fail to fit neatly within disciplinary boundaries. Indeed, I would even go so far as to suggest that the role and relevance of universities in society may ultimately hinge on their ability to organize their intellectual resources along these nontraditional lines.

But the point I want to emphasize here is that the simple—and very persuasive—injunction to firms to break down organizational walls translates into something a lot more complicated in the context of the universities.

The same is true of the prescription to concentrate on what you do best. What does it mean to say this in our context? Does it mean moving from a conglomerate to a holding company? Or does it mean breaking the university up? And in this regard, do we really understand the nature of "synergies" in university education?

And what about the injunction to focus on the customer. An unarguable proposition, as I said. But who is our customer, exactly? Our students, naturally. Their parents? Perhaps. The people who pay to support our research? Absolutely. The organizations that employ our graduates? Conceivably, yes, those too. The obvious point is that in this respect too our world is more complicated than that of our friends in industry.

THE IMPLICATIONS FOR ACADEMIC GOALS

Let me turn now to the second of the two questions I asked at the outset: What are the implications of the changes now under way in industry for the *goals* of the academic enterprise, the *what* as opposed to the *how*? The changes we have just been discussing give us only a partial picture. There is much else about the relationship between universities and industry that is also changing. Indeed, it is surely fair to say that this relationship is changing at a greater rate than at any time since the immediate postwar years. That last great change paved the way for a period of phenomenally rapid growth in federally funded science and engineering research at the universities. For forty years, the volume of federally funded university research doubled approximately every six years.

This kind of growth can't go on forever, of course, and sure enough, it didn't. It stopped in the early 1990s. And I'd be surprised if there was anyone in this room who doesn't think that this is a permanent change.

One of the reasons for it, of course, is the end of the Cold War, which, while it was under way, provided much of the justification for heavy federal funding of science and engineering. Another is the federal budget deficit. If you look at responsible projections of federal revenues and federal outlays, including entitlement programs and the interest that is due on the federal debt, it is impossible to avoid the conclusion that there will be continually increasing pressure on so-called "discretionary" expenditures—which include such obviously *non*discretionary things like food and clothing for the armed forces and maintaining roads and bridges, as well as research and development.

The forty years of growth in federally funded university research brought many superb benefits. It helped finance the education of hundreds of thousands of highly qualified and productive scientists and engineers. And it helped the research universities make many extraordinary scientific and technological contributions that were successfully applied in both the military and civilian spheres.

All of this is now in question. I don't mean by this that the postwar partnership between the universities and government is at an end. Some have suggested this, and it's true that we've had more hiccups in our relations with Washington in the last four years than we had in the preceding four decades. But most people in Congress and in the Administration don't view the research university system as being fundamentally broken, and I don't believe that they will stand by and allow the universities' relationship with Washington to unravel completely.

But it's clear that the total federal allocation for research and development won't grow by much. And when you combine this with the demands of an increasingly hungry federal laboratory system, with the deepening of the pool of first-class research universities, and with the growing Congressional penchant for earmarking, it seems inevitable that the competition for federal funds is going to become tougher and tougher.

So that is one more major change in the landscape. But I also want to mention two others. One is the decline of corporate central research laboratories, where much of the most important industrially relevant basic research has been done. Some of these laboratories have disappeared completely. And in those that remain, there is now a much greater focus on creating economic value and on developing a stronger customer orientation. There are sound reasons for this. In many cases the companies involved have come to the conclusion that not to do it would be a serious threat to their survival.

At the same time, though, the combined effect of these individual corporate decisions is to leave a worrying gap in industrially relevant basic research. Bill Spencer, the president of Sematech, recently made the point that almost every one of the major breakthroughs in semiconductor technology over the last four decades has come from corporate research laboratories but that if you look for those labs today you'll hardly find a single one.

The other major change has less to do with dollars and cents than it has to the way we understand the process of industrial innovation and in particular the relation between scientific inquiry and economic growth. The old notion of innovation as a simple, linear process, beginning with a discovery in the basic research laboratory and leading through a series of intermediate development stages to commercial prototyping and then market introduction, has been replaced by a more complicated but also a more realistic model. It is now much better appreciated that many of the most useful innovations are conceived not in a research laboratory but rather at the point of application of an existing commercial product, often by the user, or sometimes in the manufacturing process. Knowledge of markets and processes may be much more important in such cases than knowledge of the latest scientific advances.

There *is* of course a connection between new science and economic growth. But it's a connection that more often than not takes many years to develop and with unforeseen results. It's pretty unlikely, for example, that the inventors of the laser ever anticipated that the biggest commercial application of this technology would be in supermarket checkout registers.

There is also an important reverse flow of knowledge from engineering practice to fundamental science and technology. This isn't by any means a new story. Recall that it was the science of thermodynamics that grew out of the development of the steam engine, rather than vice versa. And today, among many other examples, we see high-speed computing technology playing a crucial role in solving the fundamental problem of mapping the human genome.

What does all this mean for the universities?

RETHINKING THE RELATIONSHIP BETWEEN EDUCATION AND INDUSTRY

One thing that it means is that we need a new model for thinking about our relationship with industry. We can no longer picture the research universities at the upstream end of a long chain of activities that culminate in commercialization of a new product or process, or the deployment of a weapons system, or some other such thing. I believe that it is more useful to think about the universities as serving as nodes in a national network of research and development institutions, with knowledge and ideas flowing in both directions along the links between the university, firm, and federal laboratory nodes.

This network is simultaneously pursuing fundamental knowledge for its own sake, innovation for the purposes of private wealth creation, and public missions like national defense, health, and the environment, while at the same time educating and training the next generation of scientists and engineers.

Because it's a true network, each type of R&D institution is involved in some way in all of the network's activities, but there is specialization—a division of labor—based on the special competencies that they bring to bear.

The research universities are the primary nodes for fundamental research and for education, but they also contribute to our public missions and to industrial innovation. Industry's primary role is obviously in wealth-creating innovation, but it also makes important secondary contributions to fundamental research and education, as well as to public missions.

A paramount goal of national policy, in this era of constrained resources, must be to maximize the cost-effectiveness of this network. One of the keys to this is to establish what is critical to be done and then make sure it is adequately funded. Another is to make sure that there is a clear understanding of the relative strengths and weaknesses and distinct roles of the research universities, the industrial research laboratories, and the federal laboratories, so that an efficient division of labor can be made among them. And a third is to strengthen the links between the different nodes of the network.

STRENGTHENING THE LINKS WITH INDUSTRY

And on this last point let me suggest two simple principles that I believe can be useful guides for us as we attempt to strengthen our links with industry.

The first is that we need to become world-class listeners. This is admittedly a somewhat revolutionary idea for many of us. But we must listen carefully to what our counterparts in industry are saying.

One of the things they are saying is that while they value our contributions to research, our most important contribution to their endeavors is the education of young people. Technology transfer, they remind us, is best considered the transfer of an educated mind.

Another thing they are saying is that nature of that education must change. A few months ago one of IBM's most senior technologists came to MIT to give a seminar. He described the changing nature of R&D at IBM and discussed what it means for the company's hiring policies in this area. What he had to say was interesting. The "habits of thought" that will allow people to help lead change are themselves changing, he said. Notice the interesting choice of words. Not *"what they need to know"* but their *"habits of thought."* By this he meant that they have to be more interactive. Their research agendas are no longer set by their peers but by others inside and outside the company. They must be capable of building both internal alliances across the company and external alliances with others.

IBM, he said, needs more "worldly" people in research. Another interesting choice of words. What we meant was, they don't want Capuchin monks living in a closed monastery on a hill, but rather Franciscans in the street. And in his view, this isn't what we're turning out of our graduate schools. From his perspective, our graduate students are some of the brightest people in the world, but they are encouraged to focus and define themselves much too narrowly. They get trapped by their own knowledge. He summed up by saying that in the kind of organization that IBM (and other firms) is becoming, "it is absolutely essential to know a lot of things that you don't need to know."

Other thoughtful corporate leaders are saying similar things. I hope we're listening.

The second important principle that we must keep in mind as we move to redefine our relationship with industry is to understand exactly what it is that makes us different and to celebrate these differences as a source of strength. I don't mean by this that we should stubbornly preserve all of our entrenched ways of doing research and education. But there are some who would have us become in effect an arm of industry. And when they encounter resistance to this idea, they interpret it as academic arrogance, an Ivory Towerish disdain for the world of commercial practice.

But that is often not what it is at all. Academic arrogance isn't exactly unknown on our campuses, of course. But what is also going on is that people are pointing out that the cultures and goals of the university and of industry *are* different. And a strategy that tries to paper these differences over, that fudges them, will not succeed. Just as the most stable and productive political and military alliances in history have been those in which the alliance partners understood and respected the fact that their interests did not completely coincide, similarly, a stable and productive partnership between industry and the universities must be based on a mutual respect for the differences between the two types of institutions. It is, in fact, the distinction strengths of these institutions that will form the basis of a successful partnership between them.

FUTURE RELATIONS

There is a good deal of worry and anxiety around university campuses about what the future holds. And some of this is no doubt justified. But without wanting to sound Pollyannaish about this, I think that the prospects for the research universities are actually remarkably strong and that we are superbly positioned for the future. Despite the sometimes dizzying changes that are taking place, we should not forget for a moment that the fundamental mission of the research university, the mission of continually rethinking and expanding our understanding of the world and of enlarging the horizons and deepening the understanding of our students—that mission remains every bit as valid and viable as it ever was before.

Of course things are changing. And we have to be adaptable. We should be experimenting, trying new things. And we should give up what doesn't work. But we also must preserve what does work. And we're fortunate to have a lot that does indeed work pretty well.

Chapter 4

::

Restructuring British Higher Education

Graeme Davies

::

Until this century, traditional ancient, civic, and federal universities in the United Kingdom were privately funded, usually by local sources. However, since 1919 when the University Grants Committee (UGC) was formed to advise government, nationally administered public funding had progressively dominated Britain's universities.

When polytechnics were established beginning in the late 1960s, they also received public funding as did several existing small colleges. However, funding for these nonuniversity institutions was administered locally, by education authorities in each respective region.

The Education Reform Act of 1988 replaced the UGC with the Universities Funding Council (UFC), which assumed formal university funding responsibilities. The act also established the Polytechnics and Colleges Funding Council (PCFC) to perform similar duties for polytechnics and colleges at a national level. Both councils were created as nondepartmental public bodies, giving them a high degree of autonomy and an arm's-length relationship with the Department of Education and Science (now the Department for Education).

In May 1991, a government white paper, "Higher Education—A New Framework," recommended further substantial changes. The paper's most significant recommendation advocated establishing a unitary system of higher education, abolishing the so-called binary line between the universities and the polytechnics and colleges. The Parliament's Further and Higher Education Act of 1992 created such a system and established separate higher education funding councils for England, Scotland, and Wales to replace the UFC and PCFC.

The successive reforms paralleled a marked increase in access to education. According to the age participation index (comparable to participation rate statistics in the U.S.) the number of students in Britain's higher education system grew from 6 percent in 1961 to 28 percent in 1992 (Figure 1).

THE CREATION OF HEFCE

The Higher Education Funding Council for England (HEFCE) was formally established in the spring of 1992. Thirty-five "old universities" from the UFC sector, including the University of London with its eight major institutions, were combined with thirty-three "new universities" (the former polytechnics) and forty-nine higher education colleges from the PCFC sector to form the new HEFCE sector.

Subsequently, three institutions funded directly by the Department for Education—the Open University (a distance learning institute), the Royal College of Art, and the Cranfield Institute of Technology—were brought into the HEFCE sector. Today the sector comprises eighty-one universities and fifty colleges.

HEFCE's Mission

HEFCE allocates funds for teaching, research, and capital expenditures; carries out reviews and studies relevant to higher education in its sector; and collects, analyzes, and publishes relevant information and statistics about the sector. It is the key authority responsible for deciding how higher education funds in England are distributed.

Figure 1. Age Participation Index 1961–1992

Year	1961	1970	1980	1990	1991	1992
Age Participation Index	6%	14%	13%	19%	22%	28%

THE HEFCE MISSION STATEMENT

"The mission of the HEFCE is to promote the quality and quantity of learning and research in higher education institutions, cost-effectively and with regard to national needs.

The Council's role is to advise the Secretary of State for Education on the funding needs of higher education institutions and to distribute available funds.

The Council in performing this role will:

- encourage institutions to meet the growing demand from students cost-effectively while promoting and assessing quality in teaching and research;
- encourage diversity in the provision of higher education, a widening of access and greater opportunities for current and prospective students;
- develop active partnerships with institutions, which fully recognize their autonomy;
- encourage institutions to build on their strengths and expand their local, regional, national, and international roles;
- encourage institutions to support these aims and ensure the effective and efficient use of their funds and assets through on-going strengthening of their managerial capabilities and the compilation of well-developed strategic plans."

In the summer of 1992, HEFCE formulated a mission statement (see Box) that was derived from a list of objectives developed in cooperation with the Department for Education.
HEFCE's aims were to include:

- maintaining and developing high-quality and cost-effective institutions that provide student education, advancement of knowledge, and the pursuit of scholarship; and work toward meeting national needs;
- promoting quality higher education that is distinctive in emphasizing personal development in relation to the world of work and the community;
- widening educational access to all individuals who wish to benefit and have the necessary qualities to do so;
- assessing the needs, aspirations, and concerns of the diverse range of institutions in the sector and effectively representing these to the Secretary of State for Education and others.

HEFCE would achieve these aims by:

- encouraging institutions to exercise their autonomy to the maximum degree consistent with full accountability for their use of funds derived from HEFCE as provided by the Further and Higher Education Act of 1992. (The act also recognizes that institutions obtain funds from other sources that give them increased scope to pursue their own policies and to take their own initiatives alongside activities receiving HEFCE support);
- supporting a further strengthening by institutions of their managerial capabilities to meet the challenges of a changing environment and to ensure the effective and efficient use of their funds and assets through strategic planning that addresses academic, financial, and physical plant matters;
- contracting with institutions throughout England to provide full- and part-time courses at subdegree, degree, and postgraduate levels;
- encouraging the maintenance and enhancement of cost-effective teaching, scholarship, and research of high quality, the fruits of which should increasingly be made available to external organizations and individuals in both the private and public sectors, thereby enhancing institutions' own opportunities for further development;
- encouraging arrangements whereby institutions can ensure the quality of their academic and related activities;
- supporting increased participation by students of all types, especially by members of groups currently underrepresented in higher education;
- promoting continuing education and opportunities for part-time study in order to facilitate adjustment to technological, economic, and social change and to meet individual need for personal development;
- seeking to provide a growing range of choices within the higher education sector for students, organizations, and others seeking its services, with individual institutions identifying their particular strengths and opportunities and developing them accordingly;

- assisting the development of mutually beneficial links between institutions in the sector and secondary schools, colleges of further education, and other institutions of higher education in the UK and, increasingly, overseas;
- promoting an expanding role for institutions in regional and local life as widely recognized resource and advice centers that are readily accessible to appropriate institutions, organizations, and individuals; and
- having regard for government policy for higher education and the guidance given to it by the Secretary of State for Education.

HEFCE Governance

HEFCE and the Department for Education. The relationship between HEFCE and the Department for Education (DFE) is set out in a formal agreement, *the Financial Memorandum.* Periodically, the Secretary of State for Education also delivers to the HEFCE chair (as previously to the chairs of the PCFC and the UFC) letters of guidance, which define issues the government deems important.

For example, following the publication of the government's white paper on higher education in 1991, the then Secretary of State for Education and Science sent letters to the chairs of the UFC and the PCFC expressing the government's wish for continued expansion of undergraduate access, quality audits of institutions, quality assessments of teaching, and increasing selectivity in the allocation of research resources based on the continuation of quality assessments of research.

After HEFCE was established, a substantive letter of guidance was sent to its chairman and reaffirmed the wishes described above and laid out additional broad guidance for the future. The letter defined the following imperatives:

- develop sector-wide funding methodologies for allocating teaching and research resources;
- clearly specify what institutions are expected to provide in return for public funds for teaching;
- require increased accountability from institutions about their use of HEFCE funding for research;
- secure greater efficiency as student numbers increase;
- maintain and enhance quality by relating funding to HEFCE's assessments of teaching quality;

- maintain the diversity of missions that currently exists among institutions;
- secure funding stability for institutions entering the new sector; and
- maintain institutional autonomy.

HEFCE has responded in a variety of ways. It provides advice to the Secretary on matters it judges to be important based on knowledge gained from the higher education sector and from a range of other sources in both the public and private sectors. It also produces an audited annual statement of accounts that details payments to sector institutions and HEFCE's own internal expenditures and includes a foreword describing sector activities for the year.

HEFCE and the Higher Education Institutions. Just as the DFE drafts a memorandum of agreement for HEFCE, so HEFCE crafts agreements with each of the higher education institutions it funds. These memoranda incorporate a wide range of requirements, from the need to account for allocated funds for teaching and research to the rules for capital transactions. The second part of each memorandum details the institution's specific responsibilities for allocating teaching and research funds. HEFCE periodically reviews the financial management and performance of each institution.

HEFCE also provides institutions with information on institutional governance and management (recent papers have included "Capital Funding and Estates Management in Higher Education" and "Research Assessment"), and authoritative policy circulars on subjects such as continuing education and capital allocation policy. Of particular significance are circulars issued early in the calendar year that provide details of upcoming grant allocations.

Informal, individual interactions between members of these organizations contribute significantly to the system's success. Individual contacts are made, particularly by the staff in HEFCE's Institutions and Programmes Division, when dealing with inquiries, attending meetings and conferences, and visiting campuses to discuss institutional, financial, and organizational issues. Among the most important communications from the sector institutions are those associated with the preparation and presentation of institutional strategic plans, which address academic, financial, and facilities planning matters.

The governance relationship and workflows between the Department for Education, HEFCE, and its sector institutions is mapped in Figure 2.

HEFCE FUNDING METHODOLOGIES

HEFCE distributes recurrent funding for teaching (T) and research (R) through largely formula-driven methods. In addition, it distributes non-formula funding (NFF) for activities that fall outside the normal requirements of teaching and research (e.g., special museums, research reactors) or that are consequences of exceptional circumstances.

For 1993–94, the first year for which HEFCE was fully responsible for funding higher education institutions in England, its total allocation of over 2.5 billion British pounds was divided as follows:

Figure 2. HEFCE Interactions with DFE and Sector Institutions

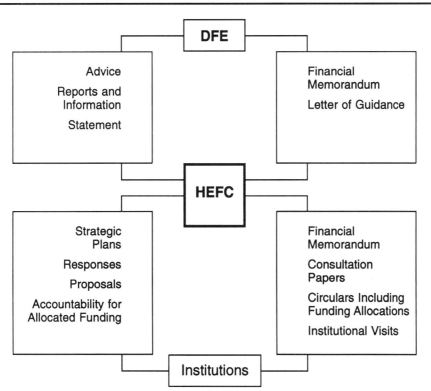

$$T \quad = £ \quad 1{,}565.1M \quad (62.0\%)$$
$$R \quad = £ \quad 6.18.0M \quad (24.5\%)$$
$$NFF = £ \quad 342.8M \quad (13.5\%)$$

The Funding of Teaching

HEFCE divides the funding of teaching into three components:

- core funding
- funding for enrollment growth
- proposal funding

The amount of the first component, core funding, is based on enrollments and provides stability by assuring each institution a predictable baseline resource level from year to year. The other two components, enrollment growth funding and proposal funding, provide flexibility by allowing institutions to make constructive changes over time.

HEFCE determines the amounts for core funding and enrollment growth funding based on a matrix of three dimensions: academic subject area, student mode, and student level. Funding data from eleven broad academic subject areas (e.g., humanities, social sciences, etc.) are combined with data on two student modes, full-time and part-time ("sandwich students," or co-op students in U.S. parlance, are counted as full-time), and two student levels, undergraduates/graduate taught students and graduate research students. (Graduate taught students are roughly equivalent to master's and professional students in the U.S.) A matrix of forty-four cells (eleven academic subject areas times two modes times two levels) is created.

The Average Unit of Council Funding. For each of the forty-four cells in which an institution is active, a key variable is calculated—the average unit of council funding (AUCF). The AUCF is the amount an institution reports spending for a particular academic subject area, mode, and level divided by the relevant number of enrolled UK and European Community students (both HEFCE-subsidized and fees-paying). Refinements are made to ensure consistent interinstitutional comparisons. Baseline AUCFs for each cell are obtained by averaging these figures across all HEFCE institutions.

All AUCFs are subjected to two adjustments:

- an increase based on the government's forecast of inflation; and
- a variable, relatively small downward adjustment reflecting desired productivity improvement.

For 1993–94, the adjustment for inflation was set at 2 percent. The average productivity adjustment was set at 2 percent with a maximum limit of 3 percent except for the quota areas of medicine, dentistry, and initial teacher training, where it was set at 1 percent with no variation. The productivity adjustment is formula-driven so that cells having larger AUCF values receive larger adjustments, and those having smaller values receive smaller adjustments. Figure 3 shows sample AUCF calculations for a matrix cell containing data on full-time, undergraduate/graduate taught students in the social sciences.

Core funding. To determine an institution's core funding level, the adjusted AUCFs for all cells in which the institution is active are multiplied by the appropriate student numbers and the result is totaled. HEFCE awards this sum as a block grant to the institution. Although it has been calculated on a cell-by-cell basis, this grant may be used as the institution wishes.

Enrollment growth funding. Enrollment growth funding is based on the number of incremental student places HEFCE decides to allocate to an institution. HEFCE encourages efficiency by awarding the highest percentage of incremental student places to those institutions with the lowest unit costs relative to baseline AUCFs. (The schools' own planning

Figure 3. Sample AUCF Calculations

Institution		A	B	Baseline*
AUCF (total spending/no. students)	817.3	917.4	767.3	834.0
Inflation adjustment (%)	2%	2%	2%	2%
Inflation-adjusted AUCF	833.7	935.7	728.6	850.7
Productivity adjustment (%)	−2%	−3%	−1%	−2%
Productivity and inflation adjustment AUCF	817.0	907.7	774.8	833.7
Incremental student places allocated (%)**	Medium	Low	High	N/A

* Total of institution AUCFs/number of institutions.
** Institutions with lowest adjusted AUCFs relative to baseline receive highest percentage of places.

proposals are taken into account at an earlier stage of the allocation process.) The distribution of unit costs among institutions within a given cell indicates wide variations and no systematic institutional pattern, with one exception—higher education spending in further education institutions. These institutions, which are similar to American "vo-techs," have consistently lower unit costs due to their different nature. Rather than create a special category for them, however, it was decided they would compete equally with other institutions for incremental student places since the proportion of HEFCE teaching funds they receive is small ($\sim$ 1 percent of total funds).

Proposal funding. To encourage particular developments, HEFCE includes a third component in the funding of teaching—proposal funding. Proposal funding covers first-year expenses of accepted proposals for core projects, which necessarily have long-term funding implications because of the allocation of additional student numbers. Funding for future years is incorporated into subsequent core funding. HEFCE invites proposals in areas it wants to develop. For 1993-94, proposals were invited that supported:

- the increase of two-year subdegree/diploma courses, particularly those with a vocational emphasis in science, engineering, and technology, and preferably programs that incorporate some content at final degree level; and
- new higher education courses in a geographical area where limited availability currently exists.

Allowances have also been made for special initiative proposals that do not have long-term funding implications (i.e., the associated funding will not later be incorporated into core funding). In recent years, HEFCE has invited proposals to support:

- improved access to higher education for students with special needs; and
- increased participation of students from ethnic minorities in teacher education.

Other initiatives considered have been in the areas of teaching and learning technology, library provision, and teaching efficiency.

The Funding of Research

Government research funding comes to institutions through two channels according to what is known as the "dual funding principle." A department's base level of research activity, including virtually all academic-year faculty salaries and the infrastructure needed for a "well-found" laboratory, is funded through a block grant determined by HEFCE. Incremental costs of particular projects—research assistants, specialized equipment and supplies, subcontracts, and the like—are funded by the Research Councils. (These councils are organized along disciplinary lines and serve a function in the UK similar to the National Science Foundation in the U.S.)

HEFCE inherited the responsibility for the block-grant side of the dual support system from its predecessor, the UFC, and is committed to maintaining it. Within the above framework, HEFCE's research allocation:

- covers almost all the costs of an institution's basic research, which forms the foundation for strategic and applied work supported largely by other government funds, charities, and industrial and commercial organizations;
- covers a proportion of the costs associated with projects otherwise funded by the Research Councils; the new arrangements for dual support introduced following the 1991 white paper mean that HEFCE funds will provide for the costs of permanent academic staff and premises required for such projects;
- contributes to the infrastructure costs of training research students;
- provides the research funding stability institutions need to establish long-term strategies essential for the attainment of excellence;
- allows for the identification and pursuit of new areas of research in advance of their support from the Research Councils and other funding sources; and
- provides resources that allow for the support of new entrants to the academic community while they are establishing their research credentials.

Research Funding Methodology. HEFCE allocates research funds (R) based on three factors:

- the quality of an institution's research

- an institution's ability to secure contract research income
- HEFCE's desire to further develop an institution's research program

HEFCE determines an appropriate amount of support based on each factor. Abbreviating these amounts as QR, CR, and DevR, respectively, HEFCE's research funding formula can be written as:

$$R = QR + CR + DevR$$

This present formula differs significantly from the process used by the UFC in two ways. First, it excludes allocations for overhead on research grants awarded by the Research Councils because that overhead is now provided directly to the institutions as part of the grants; it is no longer channeled through HEFCE.

More substantively, the present formula eliminates the previous formula's funding floor. The floor had ensured that every assessment unit would receive a minimum amount of research funding based on its total enrollment—undergraduate as well as graduate—regardless of the quality of its research outputs. The new research funding method seeks to reward excellence. Now, the fraction of faculty time that gets funded for research depends on the quality of the unit's research output and for the lowest-rated units that fraction can be zero.

In the present funding method, an institution's QR and CR values are calculated separately for each of seventy-two research assessment units—generally departments, but sometimes partial departments, groups of departments, or interdisciplinary laboratories.

QR accounts for, by far, the largest portion of HEFCE's research funding. It rewards the quality and quantity of an assessment unit's mainline research efforts. For a given research assessment unit, QR is determined by five factors:

- a research quality rating of between 1 and 5, awarded to the unit after an external peer review process (the Research Assessment Exercise, described in the next section)
- the unit's number of research-active academic staff (generally faculty) paid from general funds
- its number of research assistants
- its number of research students (generally doctoral candidates)

- its number of research-active academic staff equivalents funded by gifts

While the first factor, the quality rating, measures overall quality of research activity, the other factors measure quantity—i.e., the amount of research activity funded by HEFCE's block grant, Research Council grants, and gifts (but excluding research contracts).

HEFCE assigns weights to the quantity factors and then distributes QR in proportion to the product of the sum of these weighted factors and the institution's quality rating. HEFCE judged the number of research-active academic staff to be most important among the quality factors and assigned it a weight of 1.0. Then, using sensitivity analysis, weights of 0.10, 0.15, and 0.05 were determined for the remaining three quantity factors.

Applying the weights to institutional data resulted in the following proportional distribution:

Research-active academic staff	78.1%
Research assistants	4.1%
Research students	14.1%
Gift-funded research professionals	3.7%

In other words, the number of research-active academic staff account for 78.1 percent of the observed variation in QR among institutions, the number of research assistants 4.1 percent, etc.

CR, the amount in the research funding formula that is awarded in proportion to a unit's contract research volume, is intended to reward success in winning contract research money from industrial and commercial organizations. It also defrays a portion of the incremental overhead costs that result from this success.

DevR provides seed money for units that exhibit promise in research but are not yet able to compete effectively in terms of QR and CR. After considerable discussion, HEFCE decided that development funds (DevR) should only be available to former PCFC institutions and that its allocation should be driven by the number of research-active academic staff in those units with quality ratings of 2 or above.

In 1994, HEFCE allocated its 618 million pounds of research funding as follows:

$$QR \;\;\;= £ \; 582 \text{ million}$$
$$CR \;\;\;= £ \;\; 20 \text{ million}$$
$$DevR = £ \;\; 16 \text{ million}$$

Overall, the distribution of research funding among institutional categories left the old universities, those formerly in the UFC sector, with 91.2 percent while allocating the former PCFC institutions 6.6 percent, the general and specialist colleges 0.9 percent, and the former DFE institutions 1.3 percent. The distribution of QR was highly selective as can be seen from the distribution of QR allocations for former UFC institutions shown in Figure 4. The chart shows that 75 percent of the funding went to only 20 institutions (those shown as black bars).

THE PURSUIT OF QUALITY

Teaching Audit and Assessment

The British government has stressed the need for both quality audits and quality assessment of teaching. Audit reviews an institution's procedures for assuring performance consistency in all aspects of teaching and associated activities. Assessment reviews specific subjects, their content, and the way they are presented, examined, and supported. As illustrated

Figure 4. Distribution of QR Allocations for Former UFC Institutions

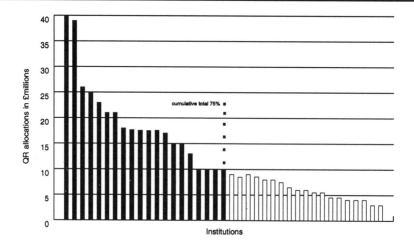

in Figure 5, audit spans all subjects within a given institution while assessment spans all institutions offering a given subject.

In 1990, as a first step toward quality auditing, the UFC universities established the Academic Audit Unit to pursue these objectives. More recently, upon the unification of the higher education system, a new body has taken over this mission—the Higher Education Quality Council.

An independent Quality Assessment Division (QAD) within HEFCE's executive office manages the teaching assessment process. The evaluation predominantly involves peer assessment. Within the QAD, there are three groups directly concerned—a core of thirty-five permanent HEFCE staff, about the same number of part-time assessors (typically faculty) on contract with HEFCE for one to three years, and 350 supplementary assessors drawn in for specific assessments.

Quality assessments are undertaken to:

- ensure that all education for which HEFCE provides funding is of satisfactory quality or better and to ensure speedy rectification of unsatisfactory quality;
- encourage improvements in the quality of education through the publication of assessment reports and an annual report; and
- inform funding, especially decisions on incremental student enrollment.

Figure 5. Quality Assessment Versus Quality Audit

Subjects	Institutions					
	Aston	Brighton	Durham	Kingston	Liverpool	Oxford
Medicine						
Science						
Engineering		**Quality Assessment**				
Management						
Social Sciences				**Quality Audit**		
Humanities						

HEFCE recognizes the diversity of institutional mission within its sector and has adopted a framework for quality assessment that encompasses the breadth and depth of the student learning experience and student achievement, examined within the context of an institution's own aims and objectives. Within such a framework, HEFCE believes that all institutions have the potential to achieve excellence, measured against the objectives that they set for themselves.

Assessment is carried out within disciplines (e.g., economics), rather than the broader academic subject categories used for funding (e.g., social sciences). The assessment procedure has three steps. First, the institution develops a statement of aims and objectives for the subject area. Then, using this statement as a standard, it performs a self-assessment of educational quality. Finally, an external assessment team conducts a site visit and delivers an independent evaluation, also based on the institution's statement of aims and objectives.

HEFCE believes that the prime responsibility for maintaining and enhancing the quality of education rests with the institution. It wishes to give full weight to an institution's own views of its strengths and weaknesses in the particular subject. Thus the second step, self-assessment, is key.

The self-assessment is made by those with greatest knowledge of the subject within the particular institution and who are in the best position to assess relative strengths in the context of the institution's own aims and objectives. It should provide an up-to-date examination of the education to be assessed. In style, the self-assessment should be self-critical and analytical rather than descriptive. It is helpful if the self-assessment draws on changes and developments in the past two to three years and has an action focus for the future, including priorities. Institutions may wish to draw on existing documentation (e.g., internal course reviews and external accreditation reports) where these are available. The intention is not to be prescriptive. However, HEFCE accepts that institutions will find it helpful to have guidance in the areas covered by the self-assessment, such as the relationship between the institution's mission and the statement of course objectives and how well each is achieved. In addition, a self-assessment might also include:

- discussion of the department's or faculty's definition or understanding of quality, informed by relevant institutional policies;
- plans for maintaining and enhancing quality;

- internal indicators of quality;
- input from students; and
- a judgment on the quality of education achieved.

Required with the self-assessment is a relevant statistical profile. The statistical indicators (SIs) should be those used by the institution to measure progress against subject and institutional aims and objectives. These institutional SIs are in addition to the set of five SIs compiled (where available) by HEFCE from national data sets:

- profile of entering students
- expenditure per student
- progression and completion rates
- student attainment
- employment and further study

Any data generated by HEFCE on the set of five SIs is shared with institutions, which may wish to provide commentaries on the SIs. Where data on the five are not available centrally, institutions are asked to provide their own data on the particular indicator, again with notes on the method of calculation and showing change over time. Here it must be recognized that the SIs do not necessarily measure performance or quality but provide background data.

The majority of assessors who participate in the institution's external evaluation are drawn from the academic staff of higher education institutions. The teams of assessors are suitably qualified and experienced both in the types of programs of study followed by students and in the subject to be assessed. They receive an induction and training program that focuses particularly on their use of the self-assessment, the proper protocol for institutional visits, and the importance of maintaining confidentiality.

As the system was originally implemented, the external review panel awarded the subject area one of three grades: "excellent" (education is generally of very high quality), "satisfactory" (education includes many elements of good practice but does not meet the criteria for excellence), or "unsatisfactory" (education is not of an acceptable quality and serious shortcomings exist that need to be addressed). However, experience and feedback have led to significant revisions in the scoring procedure. A subject area now receives separate numerical scores, on a scale from 1 to 4, for the following six aspects of teaching quality:

- curriculum design, content, and organization
- teaching, learning, and assessment
- student progression and achievement
- student support and guidance
- learning resources
- quality assurance and enhancement

Assessors then make a summative threshold judgment as to whether overall quality is satisfactory. There needs to be particular caution about the impact of the link between funding and the assessment. Where education is confirmed to be unsatisfactory, the institution will be ineligible in the first year after the assessment for any funding allocated by HEFCE for growth. It will also be informed that if quality does not improve, core funding and student places will be successively or immediately withdrawn.

The assessment year runs from October to September. Within the initial period, assessments were carried out in four areas—chemistry, history, law and mechanical engineering—to inform funding for 1994-95. By September 1994, assessments were completed in a further four subjects—architecture, business and management, computer science, and social work—to inform funding for 1995–96.

Research Assessment

Research assessment of HEFCE-funded institutions is focused around a peer review program called the Research Assessment Exercise. Introduced in 1986 and refined in subsequent years, this exercise determines the quality ratings used in calculating the QR component of the research funding formula. A panel of respected researchers from academia, industry, and government is selected for each of seventy-two assessment units, generally academic departments. At the conclusion of its review, the panel assigns the assessment unit a rating of between 1 and 5, based on the quality scale definitions shown in the box on page 69.

The panels are informed by a range of objective information, including data on publications and other "public output" of the research and scholarship process, the number of academic and support staff, the number of research students and fellowships, and the amount of external research income. In deciding what data to collect, HEFCE's overriding concern is on the information's utility for assessing research quality.

RESEARCH QUALITY SCALE

Quality is judged on a scale from 5 (high) to 1 (low):

Rating 5:
Research quality that equates to attainable levels of international excellence in sub-areas of activity and to attainable levels of national excellence in virtually all others.

Rating 4:
Research quality that equates to attainable levels of national excellence in virtually all sub-areas of activity, showing some evidence of international excellence.

Rating 3:
Research quality that equates to attainable levels of national excellence in a majority of the sub-areas of activity, or to international level in some.

Rating 2:
Research quality that equates to attainable levels of national excellence in up to half of the sub-areas of activity.

Rating 1:
Research quality that equates to attainable levels of national excellence in none or almost none of the sub-areas of activity.

However, consideration is also given to the cost of data collection and the need to keep data volume manageable for the panels.

The concept of an "active researcher" (or "named researcher" in some publications) lies at the core of the research assessment methodology. Each assessment unit decides which members of their academic staff to name as active researchers and then provides data on each person's publications and other output.

For the 1992 exercise, active researchers were asked to select their two best publications and two best "other public outputs" from work produced in the preceding three years. They were also asked for the total number of publications and other public outputs produced per year for the same period. (The period was extended by one year for the humanities to reflect the longer lead time for research in these disciplines.) The panels then assessed the quality of each unit's research outputs, based on the active-researcher data and other information described above. No guidance on interpretation was given to the assessment panels. It was assumed that the academic panelists responsible for the detailed work would know the objectives and associated standards for work in their field.

While the review panel considers the total output of all active researchers in determining its ratings, it places greatest emphasis on best outputs. Thus it might seem a department could "game" the system by limiting the number of active researchers it declares—i.e., putting forward only those having "outstanding" best outputs. The panel might conclude that these outputs were more or less indicative of staff efforts in the unit as a whole and award the unit a higher rating than it might otherwise have received. This possibility is mitigated however by the heavy weight attached to the number of research-active academic staff in the QR calculation. Departments that reduce this number therefore make a trade-off for the expected gains in average quality a more concentrated active-researcher group promises. Optimizing this trade-off maximizes the unit's funding score. Ideally, if all units do this, available funding is distributed appropriately and without the need for every academic staff member to be assessed.

At the conclusion of the Research Assessment Exercise, the panels' quality assessments are published in league tables, or comparison charts. These charts list every assessment unit in every institution and the number of research-active staff on which each evaluation was based. Levels of research funding awarded are also published. Needless to say, these tables are scrutinized carefully and used for, among other things, faculty and graduate student recruitment.

Accountability

The government clearly wants the principle of accountability to apply to all higher education institutions in the same way as for other bodies receiving substantial public funds. In particular, it has expressed a determination to ensure greater transparency in the planning and use of general research funds.

To that end, HEFCE has mandated that resources allocated on teaching-based criteria are for teaching and those allocated on research-based criteria are for research. Institutions are expected to provide, as required, information indicating how these teaching and research funds have been utilized.

Identifying the real costs linked to research is also important in the context of contract research pricing. In 1992, HEFCE and its Scottish and Welsh counterparts commissioned a report from Coopers and Lybrand titled "Research Accountability," which was subsequently issued to institutions in the various sectors for comment. The report identified seven levels of accountability, ranging from using the Research Assessment Exercise results as a sufficient measure of how well funds are spent to demanding a detailed accounting for research time and resource utilization by individual research workers. The funding councils ultimately decided that institutions would need to report how they allocate the research component of their HEFCE funding but not how these funds are actually spent—an appropriate balance of assurance that funds are correctly allocated to research without imposing expensive and time-consuming mechanisms for recording and measuring actual expenditure.

Future Policies

HEFCE identifies and examines emerging issues of importance to its sector through its Policy Division. Current policy studies, many in collaboration with sector representatives, include the following topics:

- structure and organization of the academic year
- library resources and facilities planning
- future of the Overseas Research Students Award program
- support for minority subjects
- future policy and provision for continuing education
- development of performance indicators for academic, teaching quality, finance, and estate purposes
- equipment needs and funding
- widening participation
- regional factors in higher education
- age profile of current academic staff and the consequences for future human resources planning and recruitment strategies

Of these studies, one of the potentially most far-reaching is the review of the structure and organization of the academic year. A primary aim is to identify ways institutions can enhance the use of their capital resources while recognizing that working the plants harder will require more funding for additional staff.

The study, as explained in HEFCE documentation, considers "various approaches to the organization of the academic year with a view to maintaining quality and diversity, optimizing efficient expansion, and the implications of such approaches, including cost implications for course structures, the school and further education year, and examination dates; accommodation usage, requirements and maintenance; institutional income; student maintenance; the number of contract terms of staff of all kinds; and research activity." Specifically, the study examines:

- institutional developments—planned or implemented—that change the organization of courses and/or the academic year; general resource levels including funding and staff; and the changing nature of the student body including the changing level of preparedness upon entry;
- the space constraints that may prevent institutions from accommodating additional students;
- the duties, terms, and conditions of employment of faculty and staff;
- student interests and maintaining the quality of the learning experience; and
- international developments as they affect higher education in the UK.

Chapter 5

::

Applying Contribution Margin Analysis in a Research University

Daniel J. Rodas, Geoffrey Cox, and *Joy Mundy*

::

INTRODUCTION

In the last few years as Stanford University has embarked on a number of restructuring efforts, it has become increasingly clear that we need to analyze our costs and revenues in new ways. In particular, we need to understand the costs and revenues most closely associated with our core educational and research programs. Understanding these costs and revenues is critical for assessing the trade-offs of various resource reallocation and restructuring scenarios presently under consideration. As we have discovered, the data available in the University financial accounts are not very helpful for understanding the economies driving our academic programs.

This chapter describes an internally developed financial statement—The Stanford Cost Model—that summarizes cost and revenue data in a format highly useful for understanding and analyzing academic programs. In contrast to many other cost analyses built around administrative processes or overhead allocations, the Stanford Cost Model focuses on academic activity—the primary "business" of the institution. At the same time, however, the model can be used to understand and improve certain nonacademic administrative functions.

Introduced in 1993, the Stanford Cost Model organizes traditional and nontraditional financial data in a way that highlights the underlying economics of the University's schools, teaching departments, and organized research units. The cost model is not meant to replace the standard financial accounting statements legally required for reporting purposes. Rather, the model offers a means of understanding and controlling costs by illuminating the differential costs associated with running the various schools, academic departments, and organized research units that make up the University. At the same time, the model also sheds light on the revenue side of the equation by attributing the income that accrues directly from our various lines of academic "business."

The model is based on a straightforward and intuitive concept. Simply stated, the cost model associates revenues and expenses with the activities that generate them—*before the allocation of central administrative costs that obscure the true economic standing of an academic unit.* This last point is a crucial feature of the model and explains why it is so valuable for understanding the cost and revenues directly attributable to an academic unit and for making meaningful interunit comparisons. By excluding central administrative costs, the cost model reveals each department's relative economic standing before central administrative subsidies are distributed.[1]

Presently, many of the costs and revenues included in the cost model are obscured in the University's financial system and not easily retrieved, particularly at the academic unit level. In other cases, certain important line items (such as *Net Payments for Undergraduate Teaching*) are not to be found in the University's financial systems but require development of appropriate cost allocation tools. The cost model statement aggregates these cost and revenue line-items, facilitating the ability to do interesting institutional research that previously would have been either very time-consuming or in some cases nearly impossible.

A major outcome of the model is the generation of what corporate financial analysts would recognize as a contribution margin—the

---

[1] For those readers familiar with the principles of Responsibility Center Budgeting (RCB), the concepts underlying the cost model may sound surprisingly familiar. In fact, they are both based on the same allocation principle of attributing costs and revenues to academic units before the allocation of central costs. The major difference is that the cost model is a conceptual tool, not a resource allocation method.

difference between gross revenues and gross costs. The cost model contribution margin represents the unallocated cost of managing an academic unit. It is a number that seldom appears in the lexicon of nonprofit financial analysis despite its inherent utility as a device for measuring and comparing unit performance.

As will be explained later in this chapter, the contribution margin is, by itself, a powerful financial indicator and "bottom line." However, the model facilitates other forms of valuable analysis as well. In particular, the cost model is useful for performing a wide range of internal benchmark analyses related to the following general areas:

- Committed versus discretionary costs
- Income items by type
- General activity versus sponsored research
- Net undergraduate tuition income attributable to each department's teaching efforts
- "Profitability" of graduate education

But before turning to these applications, the next section lays out the basic features and rationale for the cost model.

GENERAL DESIGN OF THE COST MODEL

Figure 1 illustrates the basic format of the model. The same format is used for all units included in the study—schools, teaching departments, organized research units, and a few other free-standing academic or research programs, such as the University's Hoover Institution, and a few interdisciplinary undergraduate or graduate programs that lack departmental status but which are budgeted as independent units.

The cost model is divided into two major line-item sections: expenses and revenues. Expenses consist of cost commitments and discretionary costs. *Cost Commitments* comprise two categories: tenured faculty compensation and space costs easily attributable to a given department or unit. Normally, neither of these line items varies with a department's activity level (at least in the short run) and therefore can be considered fixed costs. *Discretionary Costs,* representing all other department expenses, will vary with a department's level of activity. Where cost-cutting is possible, it will generally be limited to line items in this section. This division of departmental costs reinforces the notion that

Figure 1. Stanford Cost Model
(all numbers are hypothetical)

School X	Department A	Department B	Total
Cost Commitments			
Tenured faculty commitments	$2,963,836	$ 0	$ 2,963,836
Actual Tenured Faculty Compensation	2,597,274	644,921	3,242,195
Space Cost (Operations & Maintenance)	553,646	18,271	571,917
Space Cost (Depreciation)	196,105	4,255	200,360
Total Cost Commitments	$3,347,025	$ 667,447	$ 4,014,471
Discretionary Costs			
Non-Tenured Faculty Compensation	$ 105,055	$ 7,948	$ 113,003
Other Teaching Compensation	75,448	19,606	95,054
TA & RA Compensation	619,538	481,592	1,101,130
Staff Compensation	2,064,678	594,286	2,658,965
Other costs (equipment, etc.)	3,032,464	520,962	3,553,426
Restricted UG Aid	0	0	0
Graduate stipends	272,885	0	272,885
Total Discretionary Costs	$6,170,068	$1,624,394	$ 7,794,462
Total Costs	$9,517,092	$2,291,841	$11,808,933
Income items			
Net Payments for Undergraduate Education	$1,756,234	0	$ 1,756,234
Direct Payments for Graduate Education	2,496,490	0	2,496,490
External Grad Aid Tuition Income	284,075	0	284,075
External Grad Aid Stipend Income	155,000	0	155,000
Internal Grad Aid Tuition Income	400,000	0	400,000
Internal Grad Aid Stipend Income	124,000	0	124,000
Endowment Income, non-aid	456,238	0	456,238
Designated Income, non-aid	321,890	0	321,890
Expendable Gifts, non-aid	430,000	0	430,000
Federal Grants & Contracts, non-aid	45,000	1,215,678	1,260,678
Non-fed G&C, non-aid	3,000,000	1,436,577	4,436,577
IDC recoveries	245,678	678,000	923,678
Total Income	$9,714,605	$3,330,255	$13,044,860
Net Contribution	$ 197,513	$1,038,414	$ 1,235,927
Revenue Adjusted Gross Margin	2%	31%	9%

tenured faculty and physical plant are the University's core quantifiable assets, all other costs being discretionary.

These sections are further divided into sponsored research and general activity (sometimes also known as teaching and departmental research).[2] This distinction is useful for segregating revenues and expenses by funding source and necessary for avoiding distortions that might arise when comparing departments with a substantial volume of sponsored research. For data derived from the accounting systems, this distinction is simple to make. (Tenured faculty commitments is the only line item for which this information is unavailable. Here, we feel confident arguing that tenure is a commitment by the University as a whole and therefore rightfully belongs in the first column.)

Individual line items and their rationale are explained in the following sections.

Expense Items

Cost Commitments There are two ways of tracking tenured faculty salaries: commitments and actual payments. *Tenured faculty commitments* are defined as the base salaries and benefits of all faculty with appointments in a department and include commitments to faculty members on leave. *Actual tenured faculty compensation* represents the salary and benefit dollars actually paid to tenured faculty by the department. Typically, the commitments are slightly higher than the actual payments, since most departments have a few faculty members on sabbatical or other leaves each year. In some cases, however, actual payments may be higher than commitments due to payments in excess of base salary (e.g., for summer teaching). These adjustments are noted as a separate line item (tenured compensation adjustments).

Space costs are allocated to departments based on assigned square footage, derived from the University space inventory system. Two types of spaces costs are included in the model as separate line items: *Operations and Maintenance* and *Depreciation.* The Space Costs for Operations and Maintenance are based on a room's functional use, e.g., research lab or office. The Space Costs for Depreciation are distributed across departments based solely on total square footage (a more sophisticated algorithm is under development).

---

[2] Because of the difficulty in separating costs associated with departmental teaching and research, no attempt has been made to arbitrarily allocate costs by category. In essence, we treat teaching and research as a joint production process.

Discretionary Costs   The section labeled Discretionary Costs contains virtually all other costs incurred by a department, with the notable exception of indirect costs—an income item in this analysis—and some redefinition of student aid.

Discretionary costs include four categories of compensation: *Non-Tenured Faculty, Other Teaching, TA & RA Compensation,* and *Staff Compensation.* As with the tenured faculty compensation, benefits are applied to all salaries at a rate that excludes the RA/TA tuition remission portion of the benefits pool (more on this assumption in the section on graduate education). *Other Costs* rolls together all other expenses of a department, except student financial aid. *Restricted UG Aid* represents direct undergraduate aid payments allocated by departments from restricted accounts. In all cases, this line item is relatively small because most undergraduate aid at Stanford is administered centrally by the University's Office of Financial Aids. Of particular note, only *restricted* expenditures on UG aid are counted as costs. The unrestricted expenditures are implicitly considered an offset against income because these are monies the University pays itself. The cost model removes those unrestricted expenditures.

Lastly, *Graduate Stipends* measures *stipend* payments to the graduate students *enrolled in each department* (*not* RA/TA salaries). Unlike the other discretionary costs, which are taken directly from accounting information, the stipend figures are derived from information carried in the University's student information database.

Income Items

While the expense side of the cost model contains categories that are familiar and intuitive, the income side incorporates several new concepts. First, tuition has been allocated to departments based on their contributions to undergraduate and graduate education. Second, departmental income related to graduate education has been separated from income that can support the general activities of the department. Third, we have defined indirect costs as an income rather than expense item. Our rationale is that indirect costs represent monies recovered by the University for activities occurring in the departments.

The line item labeled *Net Payments for Undergraduate Education* represents income attributable to an academic unit based on its contribution to undergraduate teaching. To arrive at an appropriate dollar figure, undergraduate tuition collected by the University—net of unrestricted aid—was distributed among the departments based on student course units taught by faculty and instructors in each department. To assign tuition income, we chose a methodology based upon student course units. Simply, we summed the total tuition revenue for the University (net of unrestricted financial aid) and divided by the total number of undergraduate course units for which students registered, thus arriving at an allocation based on dollar revenue per course unit.

This method was chosen because it deliberately does not measure effort, either on the part of faculty or students. Instead, this method measures the income generated by the faculty members in each department. One way of looking at this allocation is that an undergraduate purchases a full loan of units each quarter and "buys" a Stanford degree for 180 units. In the internal market for educational instruction, students are consumers of course units in schools and departments around the University. This allocation method properly credits this income to the home department of the faculty member who teaches the course.

Although it is difficult to capture the economics of graduate education for departments and schools, we have constructed a methodology that offers a useful perspective for measuring the "profitability" of graduate education. Our methodology has several components. The first component is a line item labeled *Direct Payments for Graduate Education*. This is simply the tuition paid by students (or a grant that does not involve the University).

The other components include graduate aid income for tuition and stipends for students in each department. Graduate aid tuition and stipend income is categorized by whether the source of funds was external or internal to the University. *External Graduate Tuition Aid Income* and *External Graduate Stipend Income* would include fellowships funded through grants and contracts (such as NSF fellowships and training grants) or designated income. *Internal Graduate Tuition Aid Income* and *Internal Stipend Aid Income* represent funds from the University's endowment fellowships and gift funds. Neither category includes RA or TA salaries or tuition. The goal in defining the internally funded graduate aid income category was to count only those awards from University funds *restricted to student aid.*[3]

The other income categories—*Endowment Income, Designated Income, Expendable Gifts, Federal Grants & Contracts,* and *Non-Federal Grants & Contracts*—have been redefined to exclude graduate aid income. The "profitability" of graduate education in each department is the sum of Direct Payments for Graduate Education, Graduate Aid Tuition and Stipend Income (internal and external), minus Graduate Stipends.

USES OF THE MODEL

The previous section outlined the general design and line-item features of the cost model. The following section describes some of the uses of the model for understanding cost and income characteristics of selected academic units.[4]

Net Contribution Before Allocation of Administrative Overhead (Figure 2)

The final line of the cost model, the gross or net contribution margin, calculated as total income minus total expenses, measures the funds available to support the infrastructure of a unit. It is a discrete measure of profit or loss but in a strictly economic sense. Contribution margins can be expressed in two forms: "raw" and "adjusted." The raw margins are the bottom lines expressed as simple difference between revenues and expenses. The contribution margins can be adjusted by dividing the bottom line by revenues or costs. The advantage of creating revenue- or cost-adjusted contribution margins is that it offers a basis for intradepartmental or interdepartmental comparability. Such analysis yields interesting comparisons. Figure 2 illustrates the contribution margins for a collection of departments in a school. Note that these margins are based

---

[3] Many departments make awards from less restricted funds; these monies are counted in the cost model as *Endowment Income* or *Expendable Gifts* rather than graduate aid income. The rationale here is that these funds could presumably be used to support general department activities.

[4] All numbers used in the following tables are hypothetical.

Figure 2. Net Contribution Before Overhead as a Percentage of Revenue
(all numbers are hypothetical)

	Dept. A	Dept. B	Dept. C	Dept. D	Dept. E	Dept. F	Dept. G	Total
Revenue	$7,049,965	16,895,128	2,551,683	6,320,719	555,391	18,415,948	0	51,788,834
Net contribution	$ -408,874	2,283,363	163,162	1,541,307	-948,044	1,079,378	-20,276	3,690,016
Net contribution as a % of revenue	-6%	14%	6%	24%	-14%	6%	0%	7%

on the "total" bottom line—that is, including both general activity and sponsored research. In this particular school, contribution margins range from −14 percent to 24 percent. Closer analysis of the department financial statements could yield further insight into the wide discrepancy between the two departments' bottom lines. In looking at the individual financial statements for all departments in this school (not included in this paper), it becomes apparent that Department B has relatively little sponsored research volume, modest gift levels, and low student enrollments. Department D, on the other hand, has substantial sponsored research and income associated with its undergraduate and graduate teaching volume.

One should avoid concluding that a unit should be restructured strictly on the basis of its contribution margin. Some departments with highly negative contribution margins may be strongly valued by the institution for reasons not related to their economic performance. Examples would include departments with small major and elective enrollments but that are nevertheless regarded as core liberal arts disciplines. At the same time, one should avoid concluding that a department with a "healthy" (positive) contribution margin is necessarily highly valued. Certain high-revenue, high-margin departments might be peripheral to the University's mission. Such patterns are common in higher education where cross-subsidies tend to be the rule rather than the exception.

This exercise can be repeated between and within schools to yield an economic picture of the major cost and revenue drivers for a given department.

Ratio of Staff to Faculty Compensation (General Activity Only) (Figure 3)

How and to what extent does the administrative staff in a school leverage faculty work? Are some departments relatively under- or over-staffed? In combination with other information about school staffing, the ratio of faculty to staff compensation may suggest some answers. Importantly, sponsored research volume is excluded in computing this ratio. The inclusion of sponsored research would likely distort the interpretation of the ratio. For this sample of schools, the ratio ranges from 31 percent to 74 percent—a spread of 43 percentage points!

Further investigation of outlying ratios may suggest over- or under-staffing. It may also provide informed discussion about how various schools organize and deliver their administrative services. In some cases, this analysis may lead to a decision to pursue process re-engineering, staff consolidation, or other forms of organizational restructuring that could improve the productivity and efficiency of administrative operations, reduce costs, and perhaps even enhance the quality of delivered services.

RA and TA Expenditures as a Percentage of Faculty Expenditures (Figure 4)

At Stanford, most Ph.D. students are financially supported at least in part through research or teaching assistantships, usually under a faculty in their home department. For students, an RA or TA offers a monthly stipend and tuition remission, as well as valuable apprenticeship in their respective fields. In addition, RAs and TAs also serve an important role for faculty in leveraging their time against the multiple demands of teaching, research, and university or outside service.

Figure 3. Ratio of Staff to Faculty Compensation (General Activity Only)
(all numbers are hypothetical)

	Staff to Faculty Compensation						
	School A	School B	School C	School D	School E	School F	Total
Staff compensation/ faculty compensation	51%	42%	74%	46%	31%	62%	49%

Figure 4. RA, TA Expenditures as a Percentage of Faculty Expenditures
(all numbers are hypothetical)

	School F	School G	School H	School I	School J	School K	School L	School M	Total
RA, TA expenditures as a percentage of faculty expenditures	8%	60%	33%	90%	59%	23%	20%	7%	47%

The ratio of RA and TA expenditures to (all) faculty expenditures suggests the extent to which various schools use graduate students to leverage faculty time. At Stanford this ratio ranges from as little as 7 percent to a high of 90 percent. The ratio has implications for faculty staffing, graduate student enrollments, and internal resource allocation decisions.

Income Sources by School (Figure 5)

What are the major sources of income for the University's schools? This item provides insight into the major revenue factors that determine the way a school "conducts its business." As this chart illustrates, the percentage mix varies considerably from school to school. Examining these ratios may possibly suggest opportunities for shifting the revenue mix to reflect current programmatic or research objectives and may also highlight differential exposures to changes in the external funding environment.

Faculty Expenses by Tenure Status (Figure 6)

Most academic units can readily identify the number of faculty by rank, but the actual costs of those faculty are more difficult to pinpoint. This table provides data on the faculty expenses by major category—tenured, non-tenured, and other faculty.

Figure 5. Income Sources by School
(all numbers are hypothetical)

	School A	School B	School C	School D	School E	School F	School G	School H	Total all schools
Restricted and designated	11%	90%	57%	49%	12%	19%	19%	39%	25%
Direct and indirect recoveries	89%	10%	2%	33%	53%	52%	24%	3%	41%
Undergraduate income	0%	0%	2%	7%	6%	9%	48%	4%	19%
Graduate education income	0%	0%	39%	11%	28%	20%	9%	53%	15%

Figure 6. Faculty Expenses by Tenure Status
(all numbers are hypothetical)

	School D	School E	School F	School G	School H	School I	School J	School K	Total
Tenured faculty (actual)	60%	84%	73%	81%	94%	70%	70%	81%	72%
Non-tenured faculty	27%	8%	15%	10%	3%	23%	14%	10%	16%
Other faculty	13%	8%	11%	9%	3%	8%	16%	8%	12%

It is interesting to note that the percentage of faculty costs "locked" in tenured compensation varies from 60 percent to 94 percent across Stanford schools. Schools with the higher percentage of tenured faculty will obviously find it more difficult to cut faculty expenses. At the other end of the scale, "other faculty"—a category that includes non-tenure-track faculty such as lecturers and other annual appointments—ranges from 3 percent to 16 percent. This is a subset of faculty expenses over which schools have broad authority. In some cases, it may be financially expedient for schools to hire lecturers to teach certain courses in lieu of tenure-line faculty. In other instances, however, it may be more cost-effective to rely on the "core" tenure or tenure-line faculty to teach these courses. These are questions that school faculty and administrators must decide for themselves.

Other Applications

Numerous other comparisons can be derived from the cost model, including:

- Expenses by major category (staffing, O & M, space, etc.)
- Sponsored Research Income/General Activity Income
- Direct Payments for Graduate Education/All Other Sources of Graduate Tuition and Stipend Income
- Total Space Costs/Total Faculty Compensation
- Sponsored Research Income/Number of Faculty
- General Activity Expenses/Number of Faculty
- Number of Non-Faculty Staff/Total Faculty Compensation
- Graduate Stipends/RA & TA Compensation
- Cost Commitments/Discretionary Costs
- Profitability of Graduate Education

CONCLUSION

As the previous discussion and examples suggest, the cost model facilitates internal benchmark comparisons among and within Stanford's schools, departments, and organized research units. It provides an objective basis for understanding the economics of academic units and may provide insight into strengths, weaknesses, and opportunities for the future. Over time, as data are aggregated for successive fiscal years, it will be possible to perform time series analysis of key strategic indicators. Such longitudinal analysis will be particularly helpful for understanding whether academic or administrative restructuring actually succeeds in reducing costs or raising revenues.

One of the most important outcomes of the model it its usefulness for stimulating discussions about "What we do and why?" at all levels in the structural hierarchy—Provostial, School, and Department. When integrated with qualitative data about significant noneconomic aspects of a school or department, the cost model is an especially powerful analytical tool. The cost model can encourage substantive discussions about the quality of academic programs, the curricular coherence of undergraduate and graduate programs, and the relation of an academic unit to the broader mission of an institution.

The Stanford Cost Model facilitates direct interunit comparisons on a number of key financial dimensions, a process which may help unit managers to better understand the economics driving their research and instructional programs. For this reason, we believe the model may be a useful tool for integrating academic and strategic planning at both the central administrative and unit levels.

NEXT STEPS

The Stanford Cost Model is a relatively recent innovation and a work-in-progress. Refinements continue to be made to ensure that the model is really capturing the line items defined earlier in this chapter and properly attributing revenues and expenses. After disseminating the cost model to the University's school and administrative deans, a few minor revisions were made in the model where omissions were cited. Most of the omissions were due to "holes" in the University's information system.

Presently, the Provost's Office is using the model as one of several tools to aid the annual budget allocation process. Other factors include the relative academic strength of the department, its centrality to other academic programs in the University, its contribution to undergraduate and graduate education, and the strength of its internal planning process.

Two modifications to the model are being contemplated. One is to transform the model to facilitate "What if" marginal analysis. This would enable the Provost and other planners to understand the impact of anticipated or projected changes in cost/revenue line items associated with strategic decisions or environmental change. For example, what would be the financial impact if the Provost decided to create three new faculty billets for a selected school. How would a 30 percent decrease in income from federal grants and contracts affect a school or department? How would the consolidation of two or more small departments with similar intellectual aims alter their economies? How much would a reduction in a unit's staff or expendable faculty improve that unit's bottom line?

A last modification would be to allocate central administrative subsidies in an effort to see how this allocation affects unit economies, especially for departments with otherwise negative contribution margins. Which departments benefit most from these subsidies and how do they affect unit behavior? The cost model may help answer these questions.

APPLICABILITY OF THE COST MODEL TO OTHER INSTITUTIONS

We believe the Stanford Cost Model can be adapted by other universities interested in understanding the costs and revenues that drive their various academic units. The exception would be those research universities that presently use responsibility-center budgeting or other formulaic models of resource allocation commonly found in large public institutions. The model also would not be appropriate for highly decentralized universities where resources are not centrally allocated, although school's with numerous departmental units (e.g., Arts and Sciences, Medicine) within these institutions could adapt the model to achieve similar ends.

The basic cost model framework of revenues and expenses should remain a constant wherever it is applied. Inevitably, however, there will be minor differences in the way certain line items are defined and interpreted. Careful planning at the outset of the project will ensure the integrity—and credibility—of the final results. At Stanford, planning meetings with central administrators and representatives from the University's major schools were conducted at the inception of the project and were crucial in outlining the parameters of the model, including cost allocation methods for line items such as space and income from undergraduate education. During these discussions, it was important to address the capabilities (and limitations) of the University's information systems. Fortunately, Stanford's financial and student information systems permitted access to the wide range of data required for the project. Other institutions may find it more difficult to retrieve the necessary data, a factor that must be considered in devising a time line for the project and in planning for information system development.

Chapter 6

::

Going for the Baldrige: Restructuring Academic Programs

Dean Hubbard

::

I n 1991 Northwest Missouri State University began the process of incorporating the concepts and criteria of the Malcolm Baldrige National Quality Award into the University's planning process. This move represented an extension and refinement of Northwest's formal quality journey that started in 1984 when the University deliberately sought to apply in education what was then being tested in industrial settings. The dramatic results of those early efforts received nationwide attention and have been documented in several journals and books.[1]

The purpose of this paper is to focus specifically on the issue and methods surrounding the adoption of the Baldrige Criteria. The paper is divided into four sections. The first sets the context by briefly profiling Northwest Missouri State University, followed by a review of the planning context. The second overviews the Baldrige Criteria, noting in particular some of the conceptual and practical hurdles that must be surmounted when attempting to introduce this approach to quality on a

---

[1] See, for example, "Can Higher Education Learn from Factories?," *Quality Progress*, American Society for Quality Control, May, 1994; *Continuous Quality Improvement: Making the Transition to Education*, Maryville, MO: Prescott Publishing Co., 1993, pp. 72–89; or "Total Quality Management in Higher Education," *Developing Quality Systems in Education*. London: Routledge, 1994, pp. 135–148.

university campus. The third section outlines in some detail the specific steps followed at Northwest in gaining campuswide acceptance of the Criteria. The intent is to be descriptive, not prescriptive. Obviously, every educational institution has a unique culture that must be considered when any change is contemplated. Hopefully, enough commonalities exist so that others can benefit from Northwest's experiences. Finally, I conclude by outlining some of the University's next steps.

CONTINUOUS QUALITY IMPROVEMENT AT NORTHWEST MISSOURI STATE UNIVERSITY

Northwest Missouri State University is a typical comprehensive, coeducational, publicly supported, regional university. The University has a student enrollment of 6,000 and a faculty of 235. The majority of students live in on-campus housing and come from within a 150-mile radius of the campus. The University is located north of Kansas City in the community of Maryville, Missouri, population 10,000. The University offers ninety-seven undergraduate degrees, twenty-six master's degrees, and the educational specialist degree.

As noted above, Northwest began its quality improvement odyssey in 1984, one year before the moniker "TQM" was coined and several years before an agreed-upon set of principles for managing quality began to emerge. Obviously, quality as a concept has come a long way since 1984. Nonetheless, we began the process by systematically extrapolating from what was apparently working in industrial and service settings to our educational environment, particularly the academic side of the enterprise. By the fall of 1986, these efforts had crystallized into a strategy called the *Culture of Quality* plan for improving undergraduate education. The original plan, which has now essentially been implemented, contained forty-two best practice goals and forty action steps.

Benchmarking

Northwest's original planning process had several salient features. The first was modeled on an approach frequently utilized by industries implementing TQM: benchmarking. Robert Camp, in his book by the same name, defines benchmarking as "the search for . . . best practices that lead to superior performance."[2] In keeping with this definition, Northwest benchmarked several sources. The first was our own faculty and students. We simply asked them to submit "ideas for creating a culture of quality on campus." While different individuals and groups on campus formulated ideas, a master plan steering committee mined ideas from the numerous books and articles that had appeared over the previous decade recommending changes in higher education. By the end of the process, over 200 ideas were synthesized and incorporated into a document entitled: *Reviewing the Reviews: Suggestions for Reforming Higher Education*. Ultimately, forty-two "best practices" were selected as particularly relevant for Northwest.

Parsimony

A second important characteristic of the Culture of Quality planning process is the "principle of parsimony." Professor Nam Suh at MIT states as an axiom that "the perfect design is associated with the assemblage of the fewest parts." We take this to mean fewer and more sharply focused goals, clear definitions of quality appropriate to the task at hand, fewer administrative layers, fewer programs, and fewer evaluative metrics. Planning efforts are usually too global, involve too many goals, and fail to differentiate between the crucial and the trivial.

Northwest first applied this principle to its mission. Although six years had been spent debating the subject, by 1984 the university had not come to closure on a mission statement, in spite of prodding from the state coordinating board. Before discussing specific concepts or commitments, it was agreed that a mission statement should answer the following questions: What is the purpose of this organization: Whom do we serve? How do we serve them? What results do we anticipate? What should be the character, scope, and emphasis of the programs we offer? What elements of the university's legacy should shape or constrain the future? What philosophical presuppositions are shared regarding the nature of education and the educational process that should inform educational choices? Within two months a mission statement was

---

[2] Robert C. Camp, *Benchmarking: The Search for Industry Best Practices That Lead to Superior Performance*, Milwaukee: Quality Press, 1989, p. 12. Many current practitioners now narrow the definition of benchmarking to focus solely on processes. Outcomes are compared; processes are benchmarked.

approved by the faculty senate, the student senate, and the board, which committed the university to "place special emphasis upon agriculture, business, and teacher education, particularly as these professions contribute to the primary service region." Further, "All of the University's programs build upon comprehensive general education requirements."

Environmental Scanning

A sharpened statement of mission provided only one half of the context needed for selecting from the 200 recommendations a mutually supporting cluster of best practice goals that would reflect the basic values of the university. The Culture of Quality Steering Committee produced the second half by examining fifteen major research reports in order to identify a set of planning assumptions. Their findings resulted in thirty-seven planning assumptions subsumed under six rubrics: demographics, economics, social, political/legal, technological, and competitive. Again, the principle of parsimony was applied when, from these assumptions, five "megatrends" particularly germane to Northwest were extrapolated:

- The emerging global economy will give rise to a global community characterized by increased communications across national borders, not only in business but also in education, entertainment, science, and the arts.
- Technology will penetrate even deeper into our daily lives.
- Information increasingly will become the capital, or raw material, of economic activity. The ability to receive, analyze, and transmit information in oral, written, and numeric form will be crucial.
- The need for specialists will increase since nearly every successful enterprise operates within a rather narrow market niche.
- The rate of change in all areas will accelerate. Those who have learned how to learn will be best equipped to capitalize on such an environment.

A third application of the principle of parsimony was to the organizational structure itself. Six colleges and schools were consolidated into three colleges that more crisply reflected the commitment to "place special emphasis upon agriculture, business, and teacher education, particularly as these professions contribute to the primary service region."

Thirty-seven programs were eliminated along with five full-time dean positions and two vice-presidencies. The result was a reallocation of $1.9 million (over 6 percent of the E&G budget) away from administration and academic support areas to quality improvements in the area of instruction.

Finally, the principle of parsimony was applied to the number of areas the university would attempt to manage. The result was outsourcing the management of custodial, grounds, maintenance, and the power plant to ServiceMaster Corporation. ARAMARK manages food service and Barnes and Noble the bookstore.

Although there were sharp and sometimes contentious differences of opinion during the early stages of the Culture of Quality program, by the end of the decade it was obvious to all that this plan had resulted in major improvements in the University. In addition to the Electronic Campus, which garnered international attention, every aspect of academic life was affected. Additionally, after several years of no increases, faculty salaries grew at 150 percent of the rate of inflation despite a period of uneven and generally anemic funding from the state. Enrollment grew by 26 percent and campus facilities were also revitalized mainly as a result of the Culture of Quality plan.

In order to keep from stagnating now that the original plan had essentially been achieved, in 1991 we began to evaluate the Malcolm Baldrige National Quality Award Criteria as a possible template for continuous renewal at the University.

THE BALDRIGE CRITERIA: CONCEPTS AND STRUCTURE

The Baldrige Award was established by an Act of Congress in 1987. The award seeks to promote "awareness of quality as an increasingly important element in competitiveness, understanding of the requirements for performance excellence, and sharing of information on successful performance strategies and the benefits derived from implementation of these strategies."[3] In 1996, the award will be open to educational institutions.

When thinking about the Baldrige Criteria, it is useful to separate the Criteria's award components from its conceptual components. Giving an

---

[3] "Malcolm Baldrige National Quality Award, 1995 Application Guidelines," Washington, DC: US Department of Commerce, National Institute of Standards and Technology, p. 1.

award requires points, scoring, and some form of independent examination. One can disagree over the priorities reflected by the points assigned to different areas without disagreeing with the concepts (or seriously considering them, for that matter) undergirding the various categories, items, and areas to address. Obviously, an institution can utilize the Criteria as a template for planning without applying for the award. Many organizations apparently are doing this since over ten times as many criteria guidelines are requested each year as applications are received. Discussion here is limited to the conceptual framework and planning utility of the Criteria.

Conceptual Framework

The Baldrige Criteria are designed to expose the extent to which certain universal characteristics of effective large group behavior are present or absent in an organization. The guidelines refer to these as "Core Values and Concepts." The following list encompasses those found in the guidelines, although the wording reflects my interpretation of how the concepts best fit education. The number of items is also different because I've added "alignment"—a definite concept of the Criteria—and because I've divided some of the guidelines' items into two parts.

(1) The fundamental universal of effective organizations is a pervasive focus on the exchange that takes place between the organization and its environment; that is, "customer-driven quality." Large group sociologists and communications theorists have long described the relationship between an organization and its environment in terms of an "exchange." For-profit, not-for-profit, and voluntary organizations all seek to entice current or potential constituents to exchange their resources (time, money, or support) for what the organization has to offer. Those external "customers" accept or reject the proffered inducement based upon their perception of the benefits to be gained compared to the cost incurred. This exchange is the cornerstone of the Baldrige Criteria. (2) Leadership unwaveringly committed to quality. (3) Internal systems that are aligned to accomplish a parsimonious list of key customer-focused goals. (4) The continuous development of human resources through education, training, and support. (5) The involvement of everyone in the organization in the design and implementation of process improvement strategies. (6) Data systems that support diagnostic management by fact. (7) Assessment and feedback systems that focus on the prevention of

errors and the improvement of processes, not simply ranking and sorting (i.e., inspection). (8) An emphasis on designing quality into processes/ products. (9) Short-cycle evaluation and review systems that result in continuous improvement. (10) Quick response to indications of customer dissatisfaction and/or "out-of-control" systems. (11) A realization that expectations are constantly changing and there are no quick fixes; thus, a long-range outlook. (12) Partnerships with suppliers in recognition of the critical contribution they make to the ultimate quality of what is produced. (13) Exemplary corporate citizenship.

The Structure of the Criteria

The Baldrige Criteria looks for these characteristics under seven categories of activity: (1) Leadership, (2) Information and Analysis, (3) Strategic Planning, (4) Human Resource Development and Management, (5) Process Management, (6) Business Results, and (7) Customer Focus and Satisfaction. Subsumed under the seven categories are twenty-four Examination Items that focus on some dimension of the category being considered. For example, under "Leadership" there are three such items: "Senior Executive Leadership," "Leadership System and Organization," and "Public Responsibility and Corporate Citizenship." In similar fashion, the twenty-four Examination Items are further clarified by fifty-four "Areas to Address." Again, using the same example, the Examination Item "Leadership System and Organization" has three "Areas to Address." The first asks the applicant to describe "how the company's leadership system, management, and organization focus on customers and high performance objectives." The second asks "how the company effectively communicates and reinforces its values, expectations, and directions throughout the entire workforce." Finally, the applicant is asked to outline "how overall company and work unit performance is reviewed and how the reviews are used to improve performance."[4]

In the spirit of continuous quality improvement, the Baldrige process itself is constantly upgraded. For example, in the 1995 guidelines the number of Examination Items has been decreased from twenty-eight to twenty-four and the Areas to Address have been reduced from ninety-one to fifty-four.

---

[4] 1995 Baldrige Application Guidelines, p. 21.

Also, the titles of some of the Examination Items have been changed and some have been sequenced differently to reflect evolving emphases.

In sum, the Baldrige Criteria are generic and nonprescriptive. They are generic in the sense that, although the terminology used often reflects the argot of business, the concepts apply equally to any group. The various categories do not define quality or prescribe management strategies; rather, they are heuristic in that they force one to ask certain questions, a feature that makes the model even more powerful, in my judgment. Incidentally, Criteria specifically adapted (mainly in nomenclature) to education are being pilot tested in 1995. Northwest Missouri State University is one of the pilot sites.

THE BALDRIGE CRITERIA AS A PLANNING TEMPLATE FOR HIGHER EDUCATION

As noted above, the criteria used for selecting winners for the Malcolm Baldrige National Quality Award have been integrated into the planning process at Northwest Missouri State University. As one might expect, the initial introduction of the Baldrige Criteria for potential use on campus was greeted with considerable skepticism on the part of both faculty and some senior administrators. Objections ranged from the familiar "not invented here" to anxiety over obtuse wording in the criteria and the difficulty of extrapolating to education. Happily, those concerns have all but subsided and have been replaced with a pervasive conviction that the Criteria do provide an instructive template for evaluating and improving all facets of the University. This section outlines the steps taken that have produced these results.

Senior-Level Understanding and Acceptance

A critical first step in introducing the Baldrige Criteria on campus is to ensure that the senior administrative team understand, accept, and are enthusiastic about making the paradigm shift required. One must not make the mistake of interpreting nods of agreement and lack of open challenges as equaling genuine support. At Northwest we discovered that several steps were necessary before it could be said with confidence that the administrative team was on board.

We initially introduced the Criteria in the fall of 1991 during an all-day planning retreat involving the board, president, vice presidents, deans, and other key academic administrators. After a general introduction to the Criteria, subcommittees were asked to judge the appropriateness of each of the seven categories for university planning. While all participants were intrigued with the rigor and comprehensiveness of the Criteria, nearly all concluded that the jargon was too unfamiliar and the areas to address too business oriented for easy use in education. As a result, no attempt was made to use the Criteria during the ensuing school year. Instead, Category 1.0 (Leadership) was translated into goals and objectives that were used as the agenda for an all-day cabinet retreat. This process helped most of the participants realize the potency of at least Category 1.0 as a guide to effective leadership. This same process, which is illustrated below, can be repeated for Categories 1.0 through 5.0 and to 7.1, 2, and 3. These are all "results and deployment" items.

In the following example, the left column is quoted from the 1995 Baldrige guidelines while the right column contains the goal, objectives, and action steps extrapolated for planning purposes at Northwest.

1.0 LEADERSHIP

1.0 Leadership: The *Leadership* Category examines senior executives' personal leadership and involvement in creating and sustaining a customer focus, clear values and expectations, and a leadership system that promotes performance excellence. Also examined is how the values and expectations are integrated into the company's management system, including how the company addresses its public responsibilities and corporate citizenship.

Northwest Leadership Goal: Members of the President's Cabinet will be personally, consistently, and visibly involved in developing and maintaining a culture of quality on campus.

1.1 Senior executive leadership: Describe senior executives' leadership and personal involvement in setting directions and in developing and maintaining a leadership system for performance excellence.

Northwest 1.1 Objectives: Develop and maintain an environment throughout the University that promotes and supports quality educational experiences.

1.1a [Describe] how senior executives provide effective leadership and direction in building and improving company competitiveness, performance, and capabilities. Describe executives' role in: (1) creating and reinforcing values and expectations throughout the company's leadership system: (2) setting directions and performance excellence goals through strategic and business planning; and (3) reviewing overall company performance, including customer-related and operational performance.

1.1b [Describe] how senior executives evaluate and improve the effectiveness of the company's leadership system and organization to pursue performance excellence goals.

Consistently project, reinforce, and measure quality values throughout the University.

Northwest 1.1a Action Agenda:

Modeling Quality:

- Cabinet members will exhibit quality values in their own activities by: participating in the analysis of feedback from those who interact with areas under their supervision; leading their team in the establishment of challenging quality performance goals; regularly monitoring quality performance; recognizing, rewarding, and celebrating success in their area; and soliciting feedback regarding their own performance.
- Cabinet members will work with their team to design assessment systems that focus on prevention, not ranking and sorting.

Promoting Quality:

- The University's mission and Commitment to Service policy will be reviewed annually and revised as needed.
- Northwest's mission and Culture of Quality Commitment to Service will be prominently displayed throughout the university and published in all major documents and handbooks.
- New employee and faculty orientation will include an introduction to the Culture of Quality.
- Freshman Orientation will include an introduction to the Culture of Quality.

- Each cabinet member will review on a regular basis goal achievement in his or her area and will report at assigned intervals to the President's Cabinet and Administrative Council.
- Each cabinet member will work with the units under his or her supervision to develop and refine a plan of action for carrying out the action steps in this Culture of Quality plan.
- Each cabinet member will promote total quality management within professional organizations and groups and in those areas where his or her area of responsibility interacts with the off-campus groups (e.g., teachers, local businesses, farmers, etc.).

Measuring Quality:
- Each cabinet member will develop benchmark metrics for the primary functions under his or her purview and will measure performance against those benchmarks on not less than an annual basis.
- Focus group and personal interviews will be conducted annually to ascertain the extent to which the administration, faculty, and staff understand and support the Culture of Quality.
- Each cabinet member will participate in annual focus group interviews with students, alums, and parents.
- A survey instrument will be developed to measure reactions to each year's action agenda and

other major components of the Culture of Quality.

Celebrating Quality:
- The Student Senate will be asked to develop a recognition award to be given during the Tower Awards Recognition Banquet to the departments (academic, support services, student services) that make the greatest contribution to the Culture of Quality.
- Part of each cabinet member's plan of action will be a system for recognizing and celebrating success in goal achievement. Outstanding examples will be reported to the President's Cabinet for University-wide recognition.
- An award will be developed and annually presented to the support staff member or group making the greatest contribution to quality improvement.

A second strategy for encouraging administrative acceptance was to send the director of the University's assessment program to an American Society for Quality Control sponsored training program on applying the Baldrige Criteria in service environments. Also, an Institute for Quality/Productivity was established on campus to provide education and training opportunities for local businesses and the campus community. Through the Institute's sponsorship the President's Cabinet participated in interactive video conferences featuring all of the well-known quality gurus (e.g., Deming, Juran, Crosby, Taguchi, etc.). Finally, the item "Culture of Quality" was added to the top of every cabinet and administrative council agenda so that progress reports would provide a context for decision making in the University.

Even after all of these efforts there were still a couple of senior administrators who struggled to understand the concepts and consequently had difficulty applying them in their assigned areas of responsibility. It wasn't until we offered a graduate course in the Baldrige (which twenty administrators enrolled in) that a uniform level of what Deming referred to as "profound knowledge" could be observed. (I joined the Dean of Business in team teaching the course.)

Gaining Faculty Acceptance

During the fall 1992 semester, we began the process of seeking faculty acceptance of the Criteria. As a result of discussions involving the faculty senate president, the vice president for academic affairs, and other leaders on campus, we decided to take an exploratory approach to evaluating the appropriateness of the Baldrige Criteria that proved fortuitous in gaining faculty acceptance. Instead of charging a committee with the task of evaluating the Baldrige Criteria in their entirety and in the abstract as we had done with administrators, we decided to withhold judgment until after each Examination Item had been field tested.

In order to accomplish this task, a thirty-five member Culture of Quality Review Committee was appointed. In addition to representatives from every major academic, student, and student services unit on campus, the board, alumni, and local business community were also represented. Seven subcommittees were established to reflect the seven Baldrige categories. The membership of each subcommittee varied according to the number of Examination Items subsumed under that category. Thus, while the subcommittee on leadership had three members, the subcommittee on customer satisfaction had six, et cetera.

Each subcommittee member was assigned the task of becoming a champion for one, and only one, Examination Item. His or her task was to read everything available regarding the assigned item and its areas to address so that he or she could become the resident expert as to where and how it might be applied in the University. It was continually emphasized that the goal was to improve the University, not win an award.

The seven subcommittees were given six weeks to apply their examination items to any part of the University. At the end of that period each subcommittee and/or item champion reported to the entire group. They were to explain the components of their assigned category and items, describe the system or program within the University selected as a test site, and outline the potential improvements that had been identified as a result of applying their category. Finally, they were to indicate whether their specific examination items would add value to planning in the University. The results were unanimous. Every item champion indicated that her/his item should be incorporated into the University's planning process. Even those faculty who originally viewed the criteria and terminology as too business oriented were near passionate in their conclusion regarding the value of the Criteria for university planning. Further, while changing the words "customer" to "student" and "company" to "university" were seen as helpful for analyzing some systems or programs, the group concluded that permanent wording changes are not necessary and would probably obscure or limit the applicability of the Criteria. The only caveat sounded was that since the Criteria are so demanding and so comprehensive, a limited number of systems and programs should be targeted at any one time for analysis using this approach.

With thirty-five informed and enthusiastic Baldrige "champions" now spread throughout the institution, acceptance of the Criteria started to build. In order to leverage this enthusiasm, I wrote a series of weekly articles for the campus community that explored some aspect of the Criteria. During the spring faculty convocation I devoted my formal remarks to a discussion of empowered faculty teams and commissioned the first such team to design and implement an experimental general education program. All of these moves helped the faculty buy into the big picture.

Process Simplification

Early on we realized that if we were going to deploy the Baldrige approach campuswide we would need to develop a simple, straightforward process for implementation. It is not reasonable or even efficacious to expect every unit leader on campus to study and comprehend the Criteria. (Far better to have physicists reading and keeping up with physics than with the Baldrige Criteria!) Thus, after conversations at AT&T and with a retired executive from GE and IBM, we adopted the following seven steps planning process.

Each department on campus—including contract services—has adopted and is following this model. During the 1994-95 school year, a series of "just in time" workshops was held on each step in the model. Also, a handbook was developed to provide background information and supplemental materials. This process has been accepted on campus in part, at least, because it is nonprescriptive when it comes to defining

---

CULTURE OF QUALITY PLANNING PROCESS

1. Identify Key Quality Indicators for your areas; that is, "quality in the words of the customer." Or, what are the features of what you do that drive perceptions of quality?

2. Validate the Key Quality Indicators with your customer(s).

3. Develop goals and a strategy to accomplish them.

4. Formulate an assessment strategy to track performance.

5. Establish baseline data and track trends.

6. Benchmark superior processes at other institutions when appropriate.

7. Set stretch goals.

---

quality, determining assessment instruments, and setting goals. All it requires is that each unit on campus decide these issues for themselves.

Award Application and Site Visit

In 1994, the first year the Missouri Quality Award was open to education, we decided to submit an application. Our stated goal was to progress through the process to the point of experiencing a site visit. In order to prepare an application, we divided our Culture of Quality Steering Committee into seven subcommittees, one for each of the Baldrige Categories. Each subcommittee prepared its section of the final report. The process of preparing the report, although very demanding and time-consuming, was in itself a valuable learning experience.

Fortunately, Northwest's application did move through the process to the site-visit stage. Prior to the actual visit, I held five town hall meetings across campus to review the Criteria, stressing the "Core Values and Concepts" and the reengineering of governance that would be required. These sessions were well attended and extremely productive. Faculty and students rallied behind the process. Looking back, it is clear that the site visit was a major milepost in the University's quality journey. The campus was energized and challenged by the process. Although Northwest did not win the Missouri Quality Award in 1994 (no educational institution did), it was unanimously agreed that we would continue improving quality on campus until we finally do reach the winner's circle.

Integration into the Governance/Decision-Making Structure

The Baldrige Criteria encompass every aspect of University life. Thus it seemed logical and efficient to organize planning and evaluation around the seven categories that make up the Criteria. Accordingly, following the site visit, the Culture of Quality Review Committee became a permanent Culture of Quality Steering Committee organized into seven subcommittees, one for each of the seven Baldrige Categories. The committee was expanded to include the chairs of all the Faculty Senate committee in order to ensure cross-fertilization and communication. The primary task of the committee is to suggest responses to the feedback received from examiners and to prepare next year's application.

CONCLUSIONS

Even though Northwest has been attempting to apply quality principles for over a decade, we feel that our journey has just begun; in fact, it has just been accelerated. The agent of this acceleration is unquestionably the Baldrige Criteria. The application of these Criteria has deepened our conviction that the complex systems that make up a University in all of their diverse dimensions—from the registration of students to the presentation of ideas—can be managed in ways that maximize quality outcomes. Furthermore, while there are identifiable differences between manufacturing a product and teaching a course or delivering a service, many of the principles and techniques used in managing manufacturing quality can be applied to managing educational quality. (Likewise, some of the principles which undergird quality education have trenchant potential for manufacturing; for example, designing assessment to raise expectations.) Principles for ensuring quality that are grounded in a clear sense of mission, concern for people, and high expectations can and should be emulated in education. The Baldrige Criteria represent such a template.

Contributors

Richard Chait

Dick Chait is Director of the Center for Higher Education Governance and Leadership and Professor of Higher Education and Management at the University of Maryland, College Park. Previously, Dick was Mandel Professor of Non-Profit Management at Case Western Reserve University and Associate Provost of Penn State University. He was also Director and Education Chairman of the Institute for Educational Management at Harvard University.

Dick is a trustee of Goucher College, where he chairs the Academic Affairs Committee, and is a former trustee and member of the Executive Committee of Maryville College. He has served as a consultant to boards of trustees on dozens of campuses and on various issues, including institutional governance, strategic planning, and faculty compensation. He also serves as chairman of the AGB Trustee Leadership Institute.

His recent publications have focused on college and university boards of trustees and application of management techniques to academic organizations. These publications include: *The Effective Board of Trustees;* "Charting the Territory of Non-Profit Boards," *Harvard Business Review,* and "Trustee Responsibility for Academic Affairs," *Association of Governing Boards.*

Geoffrey M. Cox

Geoffrey Cox is Vice President for Planning and Financial Affairs at Stanford University. He was previously Vice Provost at Stanford and Director of Financial Planning & Budget and Associate Provost at the University of Chicago. Prior positions at the University of Chicago include Director for the Center for Continuing Studies, Assistant to the Vice President for Business and Finance, and Director of Benefits.

Geoffrey held teaching positions for more than ten years, most recently as a Lecturer in the Humanities Collegiate Division at the University of Chicago and as an Instructor in the Department of Philosophy at Saint Xavier College.

Since 1993, he has served on the Board of Directors of Lucile Salter Packard Children's Hospital.

Graeme John Davis

Graeme Davies is Chief Executive of the Higher Education Funding Council for England. He moved to the Funding Council from being Vice-Chancellor of the University of Liverpool, a post he had held from April 1986 to June 1991. Previously, he was Professor of Metallurgy at the University of Sheffield, having taken up that post in 1978. Graeme also spent sixteen years in the Department of Metallurgy and Materials Science at the University of Cambridge, where he was also a Fellow of St. Catherine's College.

He has held visiting professorships in New Zealand, Brazil, China, Argentina, South Africa, Israel, and India. He is a Fellow of the Royal Academy of Engineering, a Freeman of the City of London, a Liveryman of the Worshipful Company of Ironmongers, and a Deputy Lieutenant of the County of Merseyside. He is the author or coauthor of six books and more than 120 scientific and technical papers in learned journals and conference proceedings dealing with forming processes, welding, solidification and casting, and mechanical properties of metals and materials.

James J. Duderstadt

Jim Duderstadt is the eleventh President of the University of Michigan. He has held the positions of Dean of Engineering, Provost and Vice President for Academic Affairs of the University before becoming President in 1988.

During his career, Jim has received numerous awards for his research, teaching, and service activities, including the President's National Medal of Technology, National Engineer of the Year Award presented by the National Society of Professional Engineers, and election to the National Academy of Engineering. In 1990 he was appointed by President Bush to his second term on the National Science Board, where he served as Chair of the Board from November 1991 through May 1994.

Dean L. Hubbard

Dean Hubbard is President of Northwest Missouri State University, a position he has held since 1984. Prior to arriving at Northwest, he served as President of Union College in Lincoln, Nebraska. Under his leadership,

Northwest Missouri State University has received national attention for its "Culture of Quality" plan for improving the quality of undergraduate education. Northwest was the first institution in the nation to develop a comprehensive electronic campus.

Dean is internationally recognized for his work in the field of total quality management (TQM), particularly in the service sector. He is a member of the Board of Examiners for the Malcolm Baldrige National Quality Award and is chair of the Judge's Panel for the Missouri Quality Award. He chairs the Academic Quality Consortium and is a member of the American Society for Quality Control. His international experience also includes living in Seoul, Korea, and developing and consulting to language programs in six countries.

In addition to chapters, articles, and papers, Dean coauthored *The Quest for Quality: The Challenge for Undergraduate Education in the 1990s*; edited *Continuous Quality Improvement: Making the Transition to Education*; and wrote the introduction to *Keeping the Promise: Improving the Quality of Undergraduate Education*.

Richard K. Lester

Richard Lester is Professor of Nuclear Engineering at the Massachusetts Institute of Technology and the founder and director of the MIT Industrial Performance Center. The Industrial Performance Center is an institute-wide, interdisciplinary center for the study of industry in the United States and other advanced economies. His current research interests include the organization of complex technological enterprises and the diffusion of industrial *best practices* across enterprise, industry, and national boundaries.

In addition to his studies of technological innovation and industrial productivity, Richard is internationally known for his work on nuclear energy. He founded the Program on Nuclear Power Plant Innovation in MIT's Department of Nuclear Engineering. Richard has published extensively in engineering, management, and social science journals and has also contributed articles to the *Wall Street Journal* and *Scientific American*. He is also coauthor of *Made in America: Regaining the Productive Edge*.

Joy Mundy

Joy Mundy is a Managing Director at InfoDynamics, a consultancy providing services in decision support, data warehousing, and strategic information access. Prior to co-founding InfoDynamics, she developed and managed a team of consultants at Stanford focused on delivering information to support decision-making throughout the University.

Other work at Stanford has included developing investments, working with the University's CFO to refine financial policies, and helping to design the University's new budget system.

Joy has also worked as a business, financial, and investment analyst at the Bank of America and Federal Home Loan Bank.

Daniel J. Rodas

Dan Rodas is Research Assistant to the Vice Provost for Institutional Planning & Financial Affairs at Stanford University. He is also a research assistant at the Stanford Institute for Higher Education Research.

Dan has held positions at Harvard, MIT, and Tufts. In addition, he has been a teacher at the Professional Children's School and the Beekman School.

He is a member of the Committee on Finance of the Stanford University Board of Trustees and has been a member of the Dean's Internal Review Committee of the School of Education as well as a probono consultant for the Office of the Chancellor at Stanford.

His professional affiliations include the Association for the Study of Higher Education, the National Association of Colleges and University Business Officers, Society for College and University Planning, and the Stanford Forum for Higher Education Futures.